Things Thai

Things Thai

Text by Tanistha Dansilp
Photographs by Michael Freeman

PERIPLUS

Published by Periplus Editions (HK) Ltd

Copyright © 2002 Periplus Editions (HK) Ltd
Text © 2002 Tanistha Dansilp
Photos © 2002 Michael Freeman

ISBN 962-593-776-5

Printed in Singapore

Editors: Kim Inglis, Jocelyn Lau
Design: Mind, London

Distributed by:

North America, Latin America and Europe
Tuttle Publishing, Distribution Center,
Airport Industrial Park,
364 Innovation Drive, North Clarendon,
VT 05759-9436, USA
Tel (802) 773 8930; fax (802) 526 2778

Asia Pacific
Berkeley Books Pte Ltd,
130 Joo Seng Road #06-01/03,
Olivine Building, Singapore 368357,
Republic of Singapore
Tel (65) 280 3320; fax (65) 280 6290

Japan and Korea
Tuttle Publishing, RK Building, 2nd Floor,
2-13-10 Shimo-Meguro, Meguro-Ku,
Tokyo 153, Japan
Tel (813) 5437 6171; fax (813) 5437 0755

Contents

Foreword

One of the clearest, if not the prettiest, views of Bangkok is from the elevated expressway entering the city from the airport. From here, you can see the archetypal modern Southeast Asian city—office blocks, apartment buildings, hotels and a malaise of grandiose high-rise 'statements', all air-conditioned, all imported in style, all depressingly familiar. The bustle and energy are certainly here, but is this really the face of Thai culture?

But take a closer look at the passing city-scape (much easier when the traffic slows to a crawl at one of the freeway exits). Between the modern buildings are occasional glimpses of something different—a flash of sunlight on gold from a delicate spire in the grounds of a temple, a strange but elegant wooden roof, a narrow lane lined with food vendors and a woman swaying under the load of two wicker pannier baskets. Tucked away throughout Bangkok are warrens of these lanes, virtual villages in the city. Being where they are, these communities are perhaps not quite as neat and tidy as their counterparts in the countryside, but they contain much of the same traditions.

The fact is that Thailand is still exceptionally rural. Despite the migration to the cities, most Thais live in hamlets, villages and small towns, and this is where the culture has changed

least. It is also where we must look to find most of the artefacts that reflect this culture. And they certainly are there to be found—a wealth of 'things Thai' that are unique, still in production, and still being used in daily life. The water dipper, rice basket, farmer's hat, coconut scraper and the tube skirt are all products of the country's strong tradition of village crafts.

Enter any Thai monastery—easy to find, there are more than 30,000—and you find yet another world, full of distinctive Buddhist iconography represented in carvings, bronze castings, mural paintings and innumerable crafted offerings. More surprisingly perhaps, for a foreign visitor, is that these monasteries are so alive, not just with their community of monks, but as active places of worship and meditation for the laity. There are hardly any monasteries that are not an integral part of the normal daily life of the village or town.

Back in Bangkok, in and around the original heart of the city known as Rattanakosin Island (actually separated only by canals), you find a third area of Thai culture—that surrounding the royal court. This too is distinguished by its artefacts and its crafts, more refined, more accomplished and more costly than those of the country and the monastery, yet related to

both aesthetically. The Grand Palace and the sacred complex of Wat Phra Kaeo (the Temple of the Emerald Buddha) within its precincts is an exemplar of high Thai art. In the past, the best artisans were recruited to work for the palace and for the nobility, and they evolved a refined and highly decorative art in several different fields—mother-of-pearl inlay, gold-resist lacquerwork, ceramics, and many more.

However, this decorative tradition, which makes up so much of Thai artistic expression, would not have survived naturally to the extent that it has without positive support and nurturing. This occurred under various rulers, and continues to this day. Thais value their cultural heritage as much as they do their sense of national identity. Many writers, both Thai and foreign, have tried to get to grips with the concept of Thai-ness, a concept that is elusive in definition. Perhaps it even resists precise definition in words. An alternative approach, and the stimulus for this book, is to look at how Thai-ness expresses itself through its artefacts. The things Thai that follow are an oblique approach to understanding something of the national character. This selection that we have chosen, from the everyday to those conceived for special purposes, can, we believe, give a more eloquent picture of Thai culture.

Decorative Arts

Items Created for Royalty and Wealthy Patrons

In what was until recently a highly structured society, the most skilled artists and craftsmen were requisitioned for work at the royal court, and a clear distinction existed between these specialists and those who worked in the villages. They were known as *chang sib mu*, meaning artisans of the ten types, and while they may have originally been drawn from the same pool of craftsmanship, their specializations were in courtly productions, including draughtsmen and gilders (the first category), lacquerers, wax-modellers, fretworkers and fruit and vegetable carvers. To this day, a few have their ateliers within palace grounds.

Gilded lacquer
ลายรดน้ำ
lai rod nam

While basic lacquer manufacture (see pages 12–13), is mainly associated with the north of the country, the highly evolved technique of gilded black lacquer, known as *lai rod nam* or 'design washed with water' in Thai, was a product of the capital cities. It was at its best in Ayutthaya in the 17th–mid-18th centuries, and in Bangkok from the end of the 18th century.

The basic lacquer surface is first polished to a perfect sheen. The design—eventually rendered in gold leaf—is painted onto the surface with a resist, or *horadarn* ink, just as batik patterns are created. The resist is a sticky combination of *makwid* gum, *sompoy* solution and a mineral. The design outline is usually drawn onto a sheet of paper, which is then placed over the lacquer. The outline is pricked gently with a needle to create a row of dots; a bag of ash or chalk is pressed over these dots and the paper peeled away to leave a removable trace. The resist is then applied to the areas that will become the clear background—that is, the reverse of the image.

The whole area is next coated with a quick-drying lacquer resin, which is allowed to dry to the point of being sticky. A delicate, finely beaten gold leaf is laid down over the entire surface. After about 20 hours, the work is gently washed with water; the *horadarn* ink

absorbs the moisture, expands, and causes the gold leaf above it to become detached, leaving behind the gold leaf applied to the lines and areas between the resist. Since this process did not always work perfectly the first time, a considerable amount of retouching was needed.

Some of the finest examples of Ayutthayan gilded lacquer work are seen on manuscript cabinets (see pages 82–83). The detail on right from a cabinet door shows two mythical lions at play in a forest; it is also from that period. The scene above, from the Inner Court of the Grand Palace, is from the Rattanakosin period and shows an *asurawayupak*, a creature with the lower body of a bird and the torso and head of a giant (a variant on the better-known *kinnorn*: half bird-half man), standing in the Himavamsa Forest.

Ironically, while the technique of gilding lacquer came from China, it was Chinese art that was responsible for the decline of standards in Thailand. As Professor Silpa Bhilasri points out, the two conventions were incompatible, as Chinese design treated spatial elements in a three-dimensional manner. Yet, during the early 19th century, the popularity at court for things Chinese encouraged the introduction of this Chinese form of expression, to the detriment of the two-dimensional, complex Thai art.

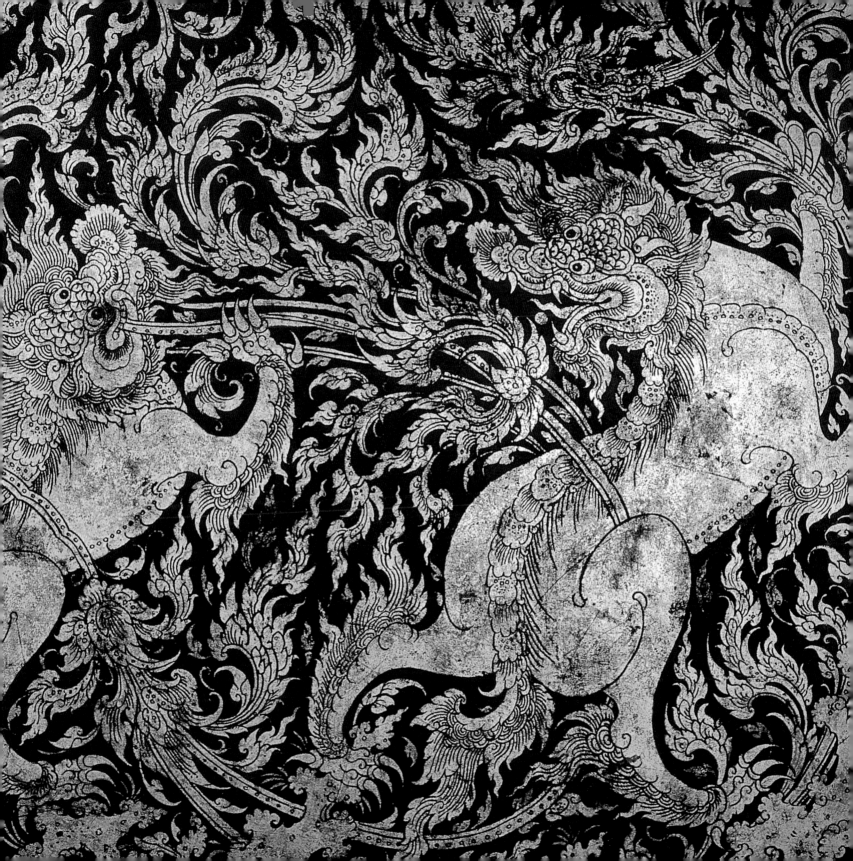

Lacquerware
เครื่องเขิน
kreung kheun

The manufacture of lacquer receptacles is among the most important traditional crafts in Thailand, being part of an almost 3,000-year Asian tradition which most likely originated in China. In its basic form, Thai lacquerware is undecorated and highly functional, although its inherent beauty may disguise its utilitarian nature. Well-applied lacquer has a remarkable range of characteristics: it is light, flexible, waterproof and hard; it also resists mildew and polishes to a smooth lustre. Indeed, it has many of the qualities of some plastics, but with the advantage of being a naturally evolved product from local materials.

Lacquer in Southeast Asia comes from the resin of *Melanorrhea usitata*, a fairly large tree that grows wild, up to an elevation of around 1,000 m (3,000 ft) in the drier forests of the north. It is similar to the Sumac tree of China and Japan, *Rhus vernicifera*.

In Thai, lacquerware is called *kreung kheun* (*kreung* in this case meaning 'works'), which hints at its origins. The Tai Kheun are an ethnic Tai group from the Shan States in Burma; after the 1775 re-capture of Chiang Mai from the Burmese, the new ruler, Chao Kawila, forcibly moved entire villages from the Shan States in Burma to re-populate and revitalize the city. This kind of re-settlement after

victory was a common practice then, and craftsmen were particularly valued. One community of lacquer workers settled in the south of the city and their name became synonymous with lacquer.

Although lacquer is often applied to wood, its original use was over a carefully-made wicker-base structure: this brings forth two of its finer qualities—lightness and flexibility. In fact, with a well-made bowl it is possible to compress the rim, such that the opposite sides meet, without cracking or deforming it.

The process is time-consuming. The form is first made using splints of *hieh* bamboo; their width and thickness must be appropriate to the object size. If they are too big, the gaps between them will be too wide to take the coating of lacquer. The best time for applying lacquer is supposedly the end of the rainy season, when the atmosphere is moist but not too hot. The resin is applied in a number of layers, each of which must be completely dry before the next coat is applied: the entire process can take up to six months. The resin, or *rak* in Thai, has varying admixtures at different stages. The first layer is often mixed with finely ground clay so as to fill the gaps in the wicker-work, while the last and finest layers are mixed with ash, from burnt rice, bone or cow dung.

Once each layer is dry, smoothing occurs, using various materials at different stages, including dried leaves, paddy husks and teak charcoal. Finally, the finished piece is polished with oil. The natural colour of lacquer is black; the red finish characteristic of Shan-style lacquerware from the North is derived from ground cinnabar, for the best quality (now rare), or the less intense red ochre, which tends to flake.

The oval box below has a rustic inlay of bamboo wedges in the shape of a flower; the eight wooden nested bowls, above, have a decorative mother-of-pearl rim. But the heights of decorative technique, practised further south in central Thailand, for the court and major monuments, are in the gilded lacquer and mother-of-pearl ware.

Opposite top: Eight wooden nested bowls with decorative mother-of-pearl rim. *Opposite bottom:* Rustic oval box with bamboo wedge decorative detail in the shape of a flower. *This page:* Oval receptacle with red finish and gilded floral decoration.

Mother-of-pearl ware
เครื่องมุก
kreung muk

Above: Two Rattanakosin-era mother-of-pearl bowls. *Opposite:* A *tieb* (receptacle with a cone-shaped cover used to offer food to monks) and close-up of same showing the intricacy of the mother-of-pearl inlay. Also from the Rattanakosin period.

A craft that probably developed in Ayutthaya as early as the mid-14th century, and which the Thais practise in a distinctive style, is mother-of-pearl inlaid into black lacquer. It is painstaking work: the individual elements are very small and lacquer-embedding involves many applications. Yet the best Thai craftsmen have gone to extremes, not just of intricate detail, but of scale of the finished objects. The best-known examples, remarkable in their execution, are the doors of the ordination hall or *ubosot* at Wat Phra Kaeo, the Temple of the Emerald Buddha, at the Grand Palace in Bangkok. From a distance they display a coherent decorative design, yet close up the decoration resolves into intricate miniature scenes; as the scale changes, so does the part played by the shifting nacreous colours. This is a hallmark of fine mother-of-pearl inlay.

The mother-of-pearl is the nacreous inner layer of the shell of some molluscs, including oysters. As with pearls, the lustre is from the translucency of the thin lining, while the play of colours is caused by optical interference. Thai craftsmen favour the green turban shell found on the west coast of southern Thailand for the density of its accretions, but because the shell is naturally curved, it must be cut into small pieces in order to assemble into flat inlay work. Even then, the pieces must be ground and polished to flatten their edges. Working with large numbers of small pieces of shell inevitably complicates the assembly process, but it also stimulates the intricacy characteristic of inlay work.

The design is first traced onto paper. Next, the outer surface of the shell is removed by grinding, and the remaining mother-of-pearl sections are cut into pieces generally no longer than 2.5 cm (1 in). These pieces are honed with flint or a whetstone to reveal the colour, and then temporarily glued to a wood backing or a V-shaped wood mount, ready for final cutting. The design is transferred to the shell by tracing paper, which is then cut into individual pieces with a curved bow saw. Removed from the wood mount, the edges of the mother-of-pearl pieces are filed smooth to fit, and pasted face-down into position onto the paper that carries the design.

The embedding process then starts: several layers of lacquer are applied to the object to be decorated, as described on page 10. While the last layer is still sticky, the assembly of mother-of-pearl pieces on their paper backing is pressed down onto it, paper side out. Once the lacquer is completely dry, the paper and paste are washed off with water.

There still remains a difference in the level between the mother-of-pearl and the lacquer, so the intervening spaces must be filled in with repeated applications of a mixture of lacquer and pounded charcoal (from burnt banana leaves or grass) known as *rak samuk*. After each application, the surface is carefully polished with a whetstone and a little water, and allowed to dry; the process continues until the mother-of-pearl is finally covered. After thorough drying, the surface is polished with dry banana leaf and coconut oil until the mother-of-pearl appears perfectly and smoothly embedded.

Not surprisingly, such a laborious technique is rarely used nowadays. Modern designs are less complex, and the mother-of-pearl is glued directly to the usually wooden surface of the object. Black tempura and filler are then used for the embedding: lacquer is often not involved at all. The pieces here, including the *tieb*, a receptacle with a cone-shaped cover used for offering food to monks, are, however, from the old school—magnificent examples of the Rattanakosin period.

Sangkhalok ware
เครื่องกระเบื้องสังคโลก
kreung krabeung sangkhalok

Some of the finest ceramics from Southeast Asia were produced in Thailand between the late 13th and 15th centuries, at the height of the Sukhothai period. The most famous site was an area of kilns a few kilometres north of Si Satchanalai, the twin city of Sukhothai. Excavation in the early 1980s revealed just how extensive the production was: this was virtually an industrial complex, with two centres close to each other, at Ban Pa Yang and at Ban Koh Noi. At the latter alone, there were over 150 kilns in a little over a square kilometre (0.39 square miles).

The ceramic production from here is now generally known as Sangkhalok ware. One explanation for the name is that 'Sangkhalok' is a corruption of 'Sawankhalok', which was another name for the area and is today the name of a small town between Sukhothai and Si Satchanalai (and which, incidentally, has a fine museum devoted to these wares). Another theory has it that the name derives from the Chinese Song Golok, meaning ceramic kilns of the Sung period. At the time, the Chinese ceramic export industry dominated Asia, and while the Sangkhalok production did not reach the same level of quality, its prices were lower. This stimulated healthy exports to other Asian countries, as far afield as Japan and Korea.

Whatever the etymology, the name stuck, not only for ceramics from the complex near Si Satchanalai but also the kilns in and around the city of Sukhothai, including a group of 50 close to Wat Phra Pai Luang.

An ancient legend has it that one early Sukhothai ruler, possibly King Ramkamhaeng, visited Beijing to pay tribute to the Mongol emperor, Kublai Khan, and brought back some 500 potters. There is, however, no evidence of this, and stylistically if there is a suggestion of Chinese influence in the designs, it is much more likely to have come from Vietnam, which not only exported pottery to central Thailand in the 14th century, but also some craftsmen.

After 1371, the first emperor of the Ming dynasty placed restrictions on ceramic export and on private overseas trade, and this sudden unavailability provided the boost that the Thai industry needed. Si Satchanalai, and a little later Sukhothai, began exporting in earnest against competition from Vietnam. Recent diving discoveries of shipwrecks in the Gulf of Thailand and the South China Sea show that this trade continued until the war with Burma in the middle of the 16th century. One route was south through Nakhon Si Thammarat, Songkhla and Malacca, another went east along the Cambodian and Vietnamese coasts.

The two kinds of kiln, cross-draft and updraft, were capable of producing a considerable range of ceramics, both earthenware and stoneware, but it is the clear glazed grey or white stoneware underpainted with designs in black that are the most closely associated with Sangkhalok. Of the two centres, the production of Si Satchanalai was superior, both in quality and quantity. The original reason for the siting of the Si Satchanalai kilns was the fineness of the local clay; Sukhothai's, in contrast, was coarse and gritty, and its craftsmen were less skillful. On the best Si Satchanalai pieces, such as those opposite, the designs are dense and well-organized, while the export pieces from Sukhothai have a more limited repertoire, often with a chrysanthemum, a circular 'chakra' or fish in the centre (see above). Tastes change, however, and the very simplicity and rapidly executed lines of the Sukhothai fish are now perceived to have considerable charm; it features prominently in modern production in this underglazed style.

Opposite: 14th–15th century lidded pots and underglaze black painted vase from Si Satchanalai. *Above:* Painted stone plate with fish motif from Sukhothai; courtesy of the Sawanvaranayok Museum.

Celadon ware
เครื่องกระเบื้องศิลาดล
kreung krabeung seladon

Celadon is named after a character in Honoré d'Urfé's 1610 play, *L'Astrée*, a shepherd who wore a light green cloak with grey-green ribbons. Nowadays the name is used to describe a particular type of (mainly green) stoneware. The hue most popularly associated with the name is a pale willow green, but in fact it ranges from dark jade to white, with greys, yellows and greens in between. The precise colour depends on the clay, the glaze, and the temperature and conditions in the kiln, which is high-fired to around 1,250 degrees centigrade in a reduction atmosphere. As one authority notes: "There has been a recent move to call celadons 'green-wares'. This is to be deplored as many celadons are not green and many green wares are not celadons." It is also worth noting that some modern chemical glazes that use copper or lead are not celadon.

In China, where it originated, it is still called green ware, and the subtly glazed classics of the technique are those produced during the Sung (Song) Dynasty (AD 930 to 1280). Some believe them to be the finest high-fired pottery ever made, on both technical and aesthetic grounds, and they have always been difficult to reproduce. Nevertheless, it was one speciality of the Sangkhalok kilns (see pages 16–17). Their best output is coloured

a beautiful sea-blue-green, and the glaze is usually rather shiny and glassy and much crazed. Since celadon glaze is difficult to control as it melts at a critical point, it was often not applied all the way down to the base, to avoid problems of it sticking to the support.

Celadon was re-introduced into Thailand from Burma at the beginning of the 20th century, and has since then, in fits and starts, enjoyed considerable export success. The centre of production is the northern city of Chiang Mai, to where Shans moved across the border on a number of occasions as part of re-settlement programmes. The Shan potters, who appear to have come from Mongkung in the Shan States, settled near the Chang Puak Gate in 1900, and began producing basic ceramic wares like pots and basins, with a rather dull grey-green celadon glaze.

Later, in 1940, when Chinese celadon became difficult to find, the Long-ngan Boonyoo Panit factory opened a little to the north of here, using the skills of the Shan potters to make household crockery. Although it lasted only a few years, it was followed by other operations, and eventually by the Thai Celadon Company. Since 1960 other factories have opened, producing varying qualities of output. It was common, even in Sung China, for

there to be a slight crazing in the glaze, and even though an increase of just a few percent in the silica content would have avoided this, the network of widely spaced lines contribute aesthetically to the depth of the glaze. The jar with ring handles on right is a Sangkhalok ware with cracked celadon glaze. The range of wares that the several factories now offer has expanded to include blue-and-white, and also white, brown and bright blue monochromes, but the core of modern Chiang Mai production remains the traditional delicate green celadon.

Bencharong ware
เครื่องกระเบื้องเบญจรงค์
kreung krabeung bencharong

The most exuberant of ceramics found in Thailand, highly valued among the nobility and wealthier commoners in the 19th and for some of the 20th century, was made in China. The motifs, for the most part, were distinctively Thai, with a cast of the religious and the mythological that included lions and divinities. The provenance, however, was not, and in these colourful, technically polished pieces we see nothing of the energetic and individualist ware from Sukhothai and Sangkhalok (see pages 16–19). There is as much reason for not considering them Thai artefacts, but in the end we do because they were chosen by the court and filled a decorative need.

Just as we see with the silk industry (see pages 30–31), overseas production–principally Chinese–was much more sophisticated than that produced locally, and it made more sense for royalty and nobility to import these pieces made to their specification than to build the necessary skills at home. The market was, after all, fairly limited. Bencharong was Chinese export ware aimed at the Thai market, beginning in the Tang and the Ming dynasties.

While the technique was Chinese, with its precise designs, rich colours and high quality over-glaze, the name is from Sanskrit (from which Thai script derives). It refers to the five colours commonly used: *panch*, meaning five, and *rang* meaning colour, reworked in the Thai idiom. The five colours were usually red, yellow, green, blue and black, although today some designs use up to eight. Bencharong ware requires several firings, the coloured enamels being added over the glaze each time. Set against backgrounds of vine and other vegetal patterns, the central motifs were mainly praying divinities (*thep*) and mythological beasts such as the fanciful lions (*singh*), the half human, half bird *kinnorn* and *kinnaree* (male and female), and the garuda (*krut*).

A variety of Bencharong, known as Lai Nam Thong, refers to the addition of gold, particularly to the rims of bowls. This addition developed to meet an increasing taste for sumptuous, unrestrained designs. Indeed, later Bencharong tended to feature Chinese designs as well as techniques.

Bencharong is interesting for what it shows of Thai taste and cultural leanings in the 19th century–the first half of the Rattanakosin period–when it flourished. As in so much else in Thai art, we can see an increasing love of decoration from Sukhothai to Ayutthaya to Rattanakosin. More than this, Bencharong reflected a royal fascination with China and things Chinese that blossomed with the reign of King Rama II (1809–1824). His son, HRH Prince Chesdabodin, directed trade between the two countries, and parts of the Grand Palace testify to the strong Chinese influence. King Rama III (1824–1851) continued the absorption of Chinese art and design, much of which can be seen today in Wat Phra Kaeo, but the decision by the Emperor to reduce foreign trade led to a decline in Bencharong imports.

This revived somewhat in the reign of King Rama V, who ordered Lai Nam Thong table-ware for the palace. However, at the same time, Rama V was forging new links with the West. Ultimately, it was the collapse of the Chinese Empire, coupled with a transfer of Thai taste to things European, that sealed the fate of Bencharong

Styles change, and change again. Today, Bencharong is deemed too ornate for most contemporary tastes, but even so the work-manship cannot be faulted. There is now some modern production in Thailand, but it falls squarely under the heading of airport art, made for tourists, and bears little comparison with the genuine old article. What the old and the new do have in common, though, is that they were and are both export ware. The difference is that the originals were made by some great kilns for discriminating clients.

Gold jewellery

เครื่องทอง
kreung thong

In 1957, pillagers uncovered the country's richest treasure trove: a hoard of gold objects interred in the crypt below the 15th-century tower of Wat Ratchaburana in Ayutthaya. Although much had been lost, archaeologists from the Fine Arts Department managed to secure some 2,000 pieces, including a spectacular collection of gold regalia, ornaments and jewellery. Now on display at the Chao Sam Phraya National Museum, the jewellery reveals the high level of gold workmanship, and the wealth associated with aristocratic life of the period. The gold button above, is one of these pieces.

The three necklaces shown here incorporate Ayutthayan gold work in modern assemblies, and all employ distinctively Thai design motifs. The leaf-shaped pendant, worked in a mixture of *repoussée* and chasing, (on left, below) is filled with wax to maintain its shape and detail, and is set with a single ruby. As remains customary, rubies (mined on the mainland principally in Burma, eastern Thailand and western Cambodia) were treated as cabochons, largely because of a regional preference for keeping as much of the weight of a gemstone as possible. The necklace on top left containing alternate gold and glass beads carries a solid engraved pendant representing a *bai sema*, the leaf-like

standing boundary stone that is placed around the ordination hall in a monastery to mark the sacred space. The opaque blue-green beads are of Ban Chiang glass. The third pendant on right, set with roughly faceted diamonds, is notable for its enamelling: this technique normally using the three colours red, green and blue, as here, was developed in Ayutthaya.

The manufacture of gold jewellery, however, did not begin in Ayutthaya. The Khmers, who controlled large parts of the country until the 13th century, certainly used gold, and pieces have been found at Sukhothai. The engraved slabs at Wat Si Chum in Sukhothai, illustrating the Jataka tales (which relate the previous lives of the historical Buddha), show figures wearing elaborate adornments, including necklaces and crowns. The 1292 inscription attributed to King Ramkamhaeng specifically allows free trade in silver and gold, although the wearing of gold was restricted by sumptuary laws to the nobility, and free use of gold ornamentation was allowed only from the mid-19th century, under King Rama V.

Ayutthayan work was the high point in the history of gold jewellery. Nicholas Gervais, a French Jesuit missionary writing in the late 17th century was of the opinion that "Siamese goldsmiths are scarcely less skilled than ours.

Opposite bottom left: Modern necklace worked in a mixture of *repoussée* and chasing is leaf-shaped and set with a single ruby. *Opposite top left:* Contemporary solid engraved pendant in the shape of a *bai sema*, the leaf-like standing boundary stone. *Opposite top:* Antique gold button found in the crypt below the 15th-century tower of Wat Ratchaburana in Ayutthaya, now on display at the Chao Sam Phraya National Museum. *Left:* Modern pendant notable for its enamelling.

They make thousands of little gold and silver ornaments, which are the most elegant objects in the world. Nobody can damascene more delicately than they nor do filigree work better. They use very little solder, for they are so skilled at binding together and setting the pieces of metal that it is difficult to see the joints."

Goldwork was revived under King Rama I in Bangkok after the defeat at Ayutthaya, and the enthusiasm of wealthy Thais for gold ornament was frequently noted by foreign visitors. Yet this very enthusiasm may ultimately have played a part in the decline of traditional Thai goldsmithing, for during the 19th century, when King Rama V became the first monarch to travel abroad, a number of foreign jewellers set up branches in Bangkok, including Fabergé. Clients with less refined tastes were catered to by Chinese immigrant goldsmiths. The Norwegian traveller Carl Bock wrote in 1888: "The manufacture of gold and silver jewelry, which is carried on to a large extent in Bangkok, is entirely in the hands of the Chinese." Today, it is in the town of Petchburi, southwest of Bangkok, that the old tradition of goldwork is kept alive by descendants of early master goldsmiths.

Silver 'bullet' money

เงินพดด้วง

pod duang

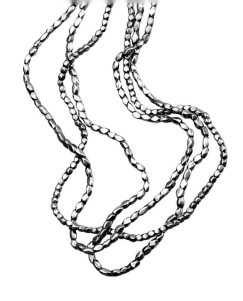

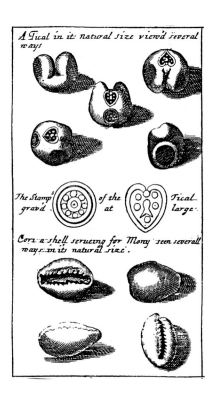

Until the 1860s, Thailand's coinage was in the form of these strange rounded lumps shown here, usually silver but sometimes gold, known in Thai as *pod duang* and rather simplistically in English as 'bullet' money. They date back to the Sukhothai period, probably introduced by the nation's first great monarch, King Ramkamhaeng, at the end of the 13th century.

They were produced in various sizes, which changed through the centuries. The earliest, at Sukhothai, were mainly in three sizes, and valued in weight: one baht, half baht and quarter baht. The baht, of course, remains the unit of currency, but in the early days of *pod duang*, it was a measure of weight. In fact, strangely, the value did not depend on the metal used: gold and silver appear to have been valued equally, except that gold's greater density meant the *pod duang* cast from it were a little smaller than those of silver.

Until 1360, anyone of sufficient means was allowed to produce coinage provided that it conformed to government specifications; thus old *pod duang* appeared in a number of different forms, and with different markings. By the time of Ayutthaya, there were some 22 of these markings, including the Wheel of the Law, Conch Shell, Garuda (as on the larger *pod duang* shown here), Elephant and Lotus.

The origin of the peculiar shape is disputed, but it is very probable that it was influenced by the form of a cowrie shell. The use of sea-shells for money, and in particular the cowrie, was widespread and by no means confined to Thailand. Indeed, cowrie shells were still in circulation in the middle of the 19th century. Simon de la Loubère's *A New Historical Relation of the Kingdom of Siam* (1693), has a comparative illustration pointing to the similarities (left), backing up the theory with Japanese gold coinage also derived from a sea-shell. Cowries were called *bia* in Thai, and the financial term for interest is *dawg bia*, literally, "that which blossoms from a shell". The hammered-in ends are certainly suggestive of the cowrie's opening. The general form could hardly have been designed for convenience, as they would have been difficult to carry around: the national dress was the sarong for men and the *pha sin* for women (see pages 136–137). Interestingly, many of the early *pod duang* had holes in them, suggesting that they were strung together. Even today, the Karen favour the smallest sizes of *pod duang* as the elements for necklaces (see pages 126–129).

The end for *pod duang* came in 1860, when King Mongkut issued a decree that the currency would be changed to flat coinage. This was

Opposite, bottom: Illustration showing how silver 'bullet' money may have received its odd shape from the cowrie shell (an early form of money). *Left:* Necklace strung with *pod duang*; many of the early *pod duang* had holes in them. *Right:* Two examples of silver *pod duang*, with the larger lower one decorated with a Garuda marking.

in response to a fairly chaotic period for the monetary system that had persisted since the capital and government had moved to Bangkok, following the disastrous defeat in Ayutthaya at the hands of the Burmese. Not only were the *pod duang* in circulation, but cowrie shells for small transactions and gambling tokens known as *pi* were also used. Meanwhile, the country had once more opened to foreign trade, yet this hotch-potch of currency was unacceptable to traders from overseas.

Foreign currency began to circulate, and indeed, from the 1850s the government was compelled to import coinage that included Dutch guilders and pesos from Mexico and Peru, often counter-stamped. This move only accelerated the demand for an internationally acceptable flat Thai currency, as Thai traders complained that the foreign coins actually contained less silver than the *pod duang*. The first attempt at flat coinage, in 1861, backfired, as the metal content was higher in value than the denomination—not surprisingly, much of it simply disappeared to be melted down.

Betel sets

เชี่ยนหมาก
chian maak

Throughout South and Southeast Asia, the chewing of areca nut wrapped in betel leaf, for its intoxicating effect, was (and still is) a custom that transcended class, evolved rituals that helped govern social intercourse, and perplexed foreigners. Early Western travellers saw only effects that were, to them, fairly repulsive: blackened teeth, red-stained lips, and an abundance of spitting that left trails of red splotches on the ground. Yet, from India to the West Pacific, it has been a habit enjoyed by millions for at least 2,000 years (that is, from its first documented use in India). The offering of betel was a sign of goodwill to guests; affection in courtships; and honour at court. The preparation of the 'quid', or a packet of ingredients to be chewed, was considered an essential social skill.

It was indeed the social significance of betel that not only surrounded it with paraphernalia, but also made the latter the focus of varied styles of craftsmanship, some of it of a very high order. The betel set on far right, in gold *repoussé*, was from the court of Chiang Mai. The open cone-shaped receptacle contained the rolled-up leaves, which, in Thailand, were served folded in this shape rather than as an enclosed packet, as was usual in India and elsewhere. The other boxes housed the sliced

nut, lime paste and optional ingredients such as tobacco, shredded bark, cloves and various flavourings. The ensemble was usually presented to guests on a pedestal tray, as depicted in the 19th-century mural at the monastery of Wat Phra Singh in Chiang Mai on right. The wooden betel tray shown above, lightly lacquered with a decorative inlay of bone, is a more modest item.

There are three essential ingredients in a quid, which combine to create a euphoric effect and are as addictive, if not more so, than nicotine. The first is areca nut, called *maak* in Thai, a hard seed about the size and consistency of a nutmeg, which grows encased in a white husk and hangs in clumps from the tall, slender areca palm (*Areca catechu*). There is, incidentally, no such thing as a betel nut: that error crept into English around the 17th century through mis-observation. The betel is actually a green leaf—the second ingredient— from a creeper of the pepper family, *Piper betle*, or *phlu* in Thai. The third ingredient is lime paste, made from cockle shells that are baked to a high temperature to produce unslaked lime, to which water is added; it is then pounded into an edible paste. Cumin (*Cuminum cyminum*) is often added to the paste, giving it a red colour.

The point of this unlikely-sounding combination is that arecoline in the nut is hydrolized by the lime into another alakaloid, arecaidine; the latter reacts with the oil of the fresh betel leaf to produce the euphoric properties. One side effect is that the saliva glands are strongly stimulated, which accounts for the large amount of spitting. The habit also resulted in the use of the flared, wide-mouthed spittoon, a common item in polite households. The characteristic red colour of the spittle—and the issuing mouth—is due mainly to a phenol in the leaf.

Nowadays, it is more appropriate to use the past tense in describing the betel habit in Thailand, as modernization has largely overtaken the custom. You are much more likely as a visitor to a Thai house to be offered a soft drink than a quid of betel to pop into your cheek, and cigarettes are now generally a more preferred stimulant. In its day, however, betel certainly had its addicts. A German pharmacologist, Louis Lewin—as quoted by Henry Brownrigg in his book *Betel Cutters* (1991)— wrote in the 1920s: "The Siamese and Manilese would rather give up rice, the main support of their lives, than betel, which exercises a more imperative power on its habitués than does tobacco on smokers."

Left: Wooden betel tray, lightly lacquered with a decorative inlay of bone. *Below:* 19th-century mural from Wat Phra Singh in Chiang Mai depicting betel being offered to a guest. *Right:* Betel set in gold *repoussée* from the court of Chiang Mai. It comprises an open cone-shaped receptacle for the rolled-up leaves, and boxes for the other ingredients.

As a footnote, it is interesting that while India is generally regarded as the home of betel chewing, the oldest archaeological evidence is actually from Thailand, where betel and areca seeds have been found in the Spirit Cave near Mae Hong Son, dating to between 5,500 and 7,000 BC.

Silverware
เครื่องเงิน
kreung ngoen

Left: Rectangular box worked in fine Thai-Chinese *repoussée* dating from the 19th century. *Opposite:* Two contemporary containers, in the traditional forms of a coconut and a lychee, cosmetic or ointment pots in a tradition of miniature fruits and vegetables, a theme shared with Cambodian silversmithing. Today, such items are often sold as tourist souvenirs.

Silversmithing in Thailand follows an ancient tradition. Votive plaques from the 8th century have been found in Maha Sarakham Province in the north-east, and silver miniature stupas from southern Thailand date to the 11th century. The technical influences reached the country from all directions at different periods, and while techniques of working precious metals were probably first introduced by Indian traders, the strongest stylistic influences have been from Burma and China. The Burmese influence was felt most strongly in Chiang Mai, particularly at the end of the 18th century when the ruler, Chao Kawila, needed to re-settle the city after its long occupation by the Burmese: as he moved lacquer-working villages from the Shan States (see pages 12–13), he simultaneously brought in communities of Shan silversmiths. Since then, the Wua Lai Road area of the city, named after the original Shan villages from the Salween River, has maintained a silver-working tradition. This has been helped in recent years by the demands of the tourist industry, but has suffered a decline in quality for the same reasons.

In Bangkok, where the mainstream of precious-metal working took place, the formative influence was Chinese. It began at about the same time, in the Rattanakosin period. The whole issue of Chinese immigration into Thailand in the 19th century, almost all from Fukien and Kwangtung, is both fascinating and uncomfortable for many Thais, for while the Chinese quickly came to dominate trades such as silversmithing, they also eventually assimilated themselves into Thai society more thoroughly than in any other Southeast Asian nation. Both Carl Bock in 1884 and M. F. Laseur in 1885 noted that Chinese were dominant among gold- and silversmiths. In fact, silver was but one aspect of the situation; Friedrich Ratzel wrote in 1876, "while elsewhere they make their living mainly as merchants and only secondarily as miners and fishermen, in Siam they control the entire economic life".

While the Chinese brought new skills where silver was concerned, particularly in *repoussée* work, their tight guild organization excluded the Thais until the two groups began to intermarry. But over the years, their techniques spread outwards while they absorbed Thai stylistic influences. Sylvia Fraser-Lu, in her book *Silverware of South-east Asia* (1989), assesses it thus: "Their work has become virtually indistinguishable from that of indigenous Thai craftsmen. They are able to produce both Thai and Chinese-inspired objects with equal skill."

The rectangular box above is just such an example of highly skilled Thai-Chinese *repoussée* work for a Thai market that had developed a taste for Western-style objects in the late 19th century. The central character is the monkey-god Hanuman, a popular mythical character from the Ramakien, the Thai version of the Indian epic tale of the travails of Rama.

In *repoussée* work, sheet metal is punched and hammered from the inside to produce a relief decoration. It is first coated in oil and then worked face down on a bed of resin. As constant hammering weakens the silver structurally, the piece being worked must periodically be annealed through reheating. This process forms a residue of black oxide, which must then be removed in a pickling solution of dilute acid. This procedure may have to be repeated several times, depending on the complexity and relief of the design. The background here has been accentuated by punching down from the front, in a procedure known as chasing.

Thai silk

ผ้าไหมไทย

pha mai thai

Left: Fur trimmed silk jacket with rich brocade. Below: Most of Thailand's silkworms are raised on the Korat Plateau in the northeast. Opposite: Three swatches of Thai silk, ably illustrating the richness, colour and intricacy of modern-day silk production in the country.

Thailand's fame as a silk producer is, perhaps surprisingly, a very recent phenomenon. To be sure, it has ancient origins—archaeologists have discovered 3,000-year old silk in the ruins of Ban Chiang, widely considered to be the earliest civilization in Southeast Asia—but until the 1950s silk-weaving was moribund.

Silk is the filament produced by the caterpillars of a type of moth that feeds on the mulberry bush. Silkworms are not, in fact, worms; they spin their cocoons using their salivary glands at the time when they change from larvae into pupae. The silk from Thailand's caterpillars, most of which are raised on the Korat Plateau in the country's northeast, varies in colour from pale gold to very pale green. Each cocoon is woven from a single thread that is 500–1,500 m (1,640–4,920 ft) long. One filament is too thin to use alone so many threads are combined to make a thicker, more practical fibre.

The sheen of woven silk cloth—its most admired quality—comes from the structure of the fibres, which are triangular in cross-section and so reflect light like prisms. It also has layers of protein that adds lustre and smoothness to its natural sheen. At the same time, this insect fibre is immensely strong for its light weight, and both elastic and supple.

The technique of producing fabric from silk is credited to the Chinese who closely guarded the secret of silk-weaving for centuries. China dominated production with its smooth, satiny cloth, and the importance of the trade in it gave rise to the overland route known as the Silk Road. The export of cocoons, silkworm eggs and mulberry seeds was banned, but eventually and inevitably some cocoons were smuggled out of China, and the techniques as well.

Silk production then spread to other Asian countries, including Thailand. Evidence from the Ban Chiang excavations, however, suggests the possibility that there was independent production in ancient times. As a cottage industry in Thailand, it dates back some hundreds of years. In contrast to the refinement of ancient Chinese silk, the Thai cloth has a relatively coarse texture with uneven, slightly knotty threads, even though the silk itself is usually soft. This quality makes it extremely suitable for hand weaving, and while modern techniques allow perfectly smooth silk to be made, the type most commonly associated with Thai production is relatively coarse and thick, with what is known as a 'nubby' appearance. This imperfection gives it a special beauty, and is immediate evidence of its hand-made nature— a welcome contrast to machine-woven silk.

In 1902 the King, Rama V, decided to raise the quality of Thai silk, and invited a team of Japanese sericulture experts to help improve the production of raw silk. A school was opened in Korat and a silk-worm breeding establishment in Buriram; new Japanese looms were imported. Unfortunately, the natural conservatism of the villagers proved impossible to overcome, and the experiment was abandoned. Then, shortly after World War II, Jim Thompson, an American former intelligence officer, settled in Thailand and set up a commercial operation in Bangkok. His company was asked to make the costumes for the original Broadway production of 'The King and I'. The boom in Thailand's tourist industry ensured an ever-growing demand. Today, the largest hand-weaving silk facility in the world is in Pakthongchai, in the northeast.

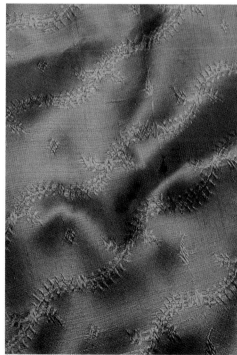

Dressing tables and cabinets
คันฉ่อง, ตู้
khan chong, tu

Traditional Thai household life was spent mostly on the floor. Kept spotlessly clean and sometimes covered with mats, the floor itself thus took the place of certain basic items of furniture, and obviated the need for others. In former times, such furniture as existed would have been restricted to storage units such as chests and small cabinets, mirrors, screens and couches, all made of wood. Very little furniture has survived from the Ayutthaya period, and none from the Sukhothai period; the oldest pieces one is likely to see are from the 19th century—the Rattanakosin period.

However, changes were taking place during the 19th century, particularly under the reign of King Rama V (1868–1910) who encouraged modernization and the influence of European styles and customs. Naturally, these changes at first affected only the wealthier Thais who had the closest contact with the court, but they then began to separate the basic customs of the upper classes from those of most of the population.

The furniture shown here, all from the Rattanakosin period, illustrates this gradual change of lifestyle. The dressing table with mirror on far right, heavily decorated and on a low matching bench, is clearly designed to be used from floor level. Note the fixed angle,

supported by the bodies of two *naga* serpents, to suit the position of a woman sitting on the floor. Nevertheless, while its decoration is fully Thai, this item of furniture is Chinese in origin. Indeed, almost all domestic furniture in what is now thought of as a traditional Thai style is influenced by Chinese models. This can be seen, for example, in the re-curved feet, in feet with a lion's paw motif, and in corner decorations of beds and benches. During the Second Reign, from 1809 to 1824, the King was heavily influenced by Chinese design ideas (see the parts of the Grand Palace built during this period). This continued in the Third, and, to a lesser extent, in the Fourth Reigns. Pure Thai style in furniture appears to have been restricted to ecclesiastical items such as the scripture chests and cabinets shown on pages 82–83.

The changes ushered in by King Rama V brought a second layer of influence on furnishings and lifestyle, from Europe, and the cabinets pictured here show the hybrid combination of Western and Chinese motifs translated into a Thai idiom. The effect was ornate and fussy, but that was entirely in keeping with their purpose—new to the Thais—of displaying personal and treasured possessions. This itself was the chief European

import, the idea of collecting objects to show off in the home to visitors, and it naturally demanded glass panels.

Cabinets are known in Thai after the style of their legs, and there are four basic types. One is *tu kha mu*, or 'pig's trotter' in which the legs are straight (and in actual fact not very much like a trotter); another, shown above, has inward curving legs, known as *tu kha khu*; a third is *tu kha singh* ('lion's legs'), which have double-curved legs, the feet being realistically claw-like and often clutching a ball (as in all three cabinets on left); the fourth is *tu than singh*, also with lion's feet but in addition a panelled base with concave grips for moving it.

Opposite and above: Four cabinets from the Rattanakosin period that would have been used for storing household items. *Right:* Heavily decorated dressing table with mirror, also from the Rattanakosin period. Chinese in origin, the mirror is kept at a fixed angle by two carved *naga* serpents.

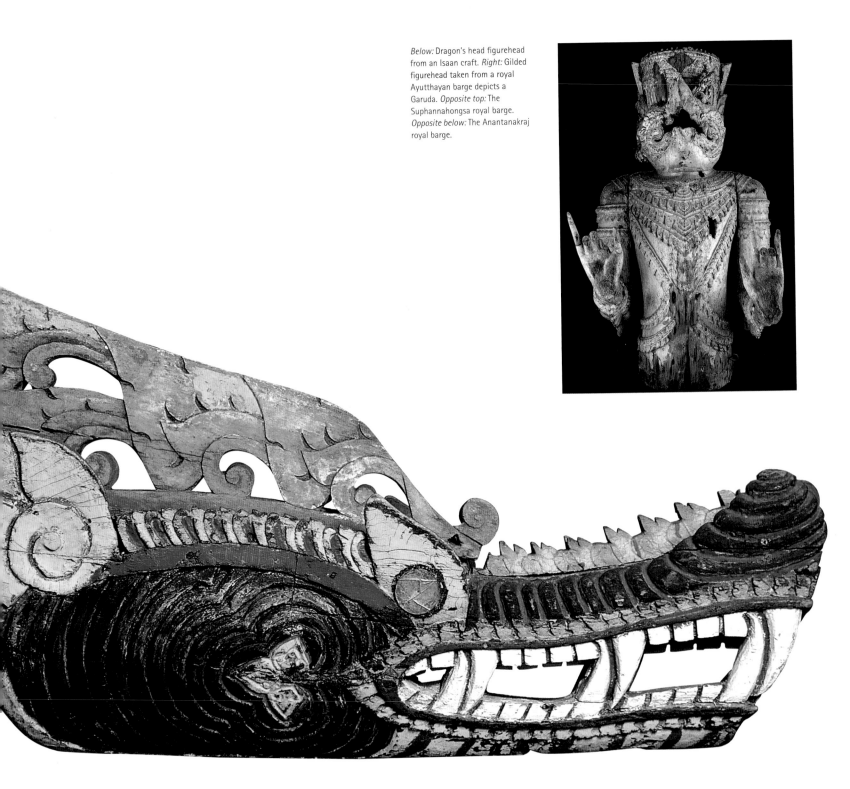

Below: Dragon's head figurehead from an Isaan craft. *Right:* Gilded figurehead taken from a royal Ayutthayan barge depicts a Garuda. *Opposite top:* The Suphannahongsa royal barge. *Opposite below:* The Anantanakraj royal barge.

Boat figureheads
หัวเรือ
hua reau

Water and boats played a prominent part in Thai daily life. Early European visitors repeatedly stressed the aquatic life in the delta and central plains. Frederick Neale, who lived in Siam in the middle of the 19th century, calculated that Bangkok had some 70,000 floating houses and an aquatic population of around 350,000. Sir John Bowring wrote in 1857: "Such is the facility which practice gives to this almost amphibious people, that the canoes are generally entrusted to the care of a child not above ten years of age, and that child a girl."

Even today, the narrow-hulled long-tail boats (named for the extended propeller shaft that allows the propeller to be lifted quickly to avoid patches of water hyacinth and other debris in the water) screaming noisily up and down the Chao Phraya River, trains of massive rice barges plying between the Central Plains and Bangkok's port, and the occasional flat-bottomed canoe selling hot steaming noodles, give some of the flavour of Thai water life. One feature of the boats—the figurehead—is worth mentioning. As elsewhere, the figurehead establishes the personality of a vessel, and is a symbol of the authority of its owner; it also protects the boat's passage through the water.

The wet season, when the waters rise, is the time for boat races and processions in some parts of the country, such as Pichit and Nan, and on the Mekong River in Issaan, the Lao-speaking North East. This brightly painted dragon's head with large mirror eyes, on left below, is from an Issaan craft. Its fierce, raw energy makes it look perfectly capable of slicing confidently through the swollen monsoon waters. The more formal and important gilded figurehead, inset on left, is from a royal Ayutthayan barge, and is the man-bird Garuda from Hindu mythology, the steed of the god Vishnu; its association with royalty makes it the long-standing Thai symbol of ruling authority.

At the height of Ayutthaya's power in the late 17th or early 18th century, royal barge processions took place on a fantastic scale: apparently, processions of hundreds of boats were not unusual. Jeremias van Vliet, a Dutch trader living in the city, reckoned that up to 25,000 people could be involved; another eye-witness, Jean Albert de Mandelslo, recorded in 1727 that "the royal escort consisted of up to 400 personal guards in seven to eight barges rowed by a hundred people each, followed by 1,000 to 1,200 noblemen, each with several barges beautifully gilded and some especially catered for musicians".

Ayutthaya fell to the Burmese in 1767. The capital was moved to Thonburi and later Bangkok, but in 1982, the pageantry of royal barge processions was revived, and continues today. One of the most famous and elaborate of the current fleet of royal craft is the boat shown below, called Anantanakraj. The seven-headed figurehead is the *naga* Ananta, who supported Vishnu on the cosmic ocean (see pages 92–93). This is as grand as boat decoration gets, but if you look carefully at the regular river traffic in Bangkok, and especially at the long-tailed boats ferrying passengers across the Chao Phraya and along the canals on the Thonburi side, you will see a bouquet of brightly coloured cloth, flowers and incense sticks tied to the prow. This is the protective *mae yanang*, an offering to the water guardian spirit, and is as much a part of the craft as is the figurehead.

Elephants

ช้าง

chang

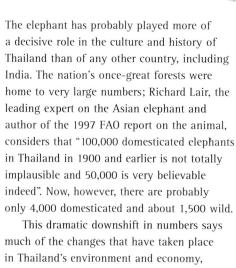

The elephant has probably played more of a decisive role in the culture and history of Thailand than of any other country, including India. The nation's once-great forests were home to very large numbers; Richard Lair, the leading expert on the Asian elephant and author of the 1997 FAO report on the animal, considers that "100,000 domesticated elephants in Thailand in 1900 and earlier is not totally implausible and 50,000 is very believable indeed". Now, however, there are probably only 4,000 domesticated and about 1,500 wild.

This dramatic downshift in numbers says much of the changes that have taken place in Thailand's environment and economy, with teak logging now illegal and most of the forests denuded, but the elephant's place in traditions remains strong. Thailand also stands unique in Asia for the extremely high proportion of domesticated to wild elephants, reinforcing the claim that the elephant has entered the culture more strongly than elsewhere. In the words of Lair: "The elephant once totally penetrated the Thai cosmos."

A white elephant on a red ground was the Siamese flag until 1917; the first known Thai inscription, from 1292, records King Ramkamhaeng's combat on elephant-back. The white elephant, which is by right the property of the monarch, and over which wars have been fought, has a significance reaching back to the legendary birth of the Buddha. According to the scriptures, he was born into the Shakya clan to Queen Maya, and "just before her conception she had a dream. A white king elephant seemed to enter her body, but without causing her any pain".

So, for reasons of religion, culture and familiarity, the elephant has featured as a key Thai icon. Images of elephants abound. One of the most famous is the 15 cm high (6 in) gold elephant encrusted with gems shown on right, dating from 1454 and discovered as part of a gold hoard in 1957 in the crypt below the main tower of Wat Ratchaburana in Ayutthaya, having survived the 1767 sacking of the former capital by the Burmese. The other elephant models here are votive pieces.

White elephants, incidentally, are rarely if ever white in colour. There may be traces of albinism, such as pale eyes and pink patches, but the true definition depends on an arcane set of distinguishing features that can be determined only by a few experts, whose deliberations take a considerable time. The Thai expression is actually 'special elephant'. At the time of writing there are 11 such animals in the country, all owned by the King.

Ivory chedi seals

งาประทับ

nga pratab

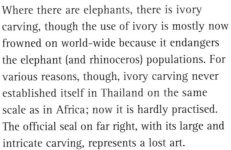

Where there are elephants, there is ivory carving, though the use of ivory is mostly now frowned on world-wide because it endangers the elephant (and rhinoceros) populations. For various reasons, though, ivory carving never established itself in Thailand on the same scale as in Africa; now it is hardly practised. The official seal on far right, with its large and intricate carving, represents a lost art.

One reason why ivory assumed only a minor importance is that visible tusks only sometimes grow in the male Asian elephant. Some males and even females, called *sidor*, have hidden tusks of about 3 cm (1 in) long, that do not protrude beyond the lips: these were of little use to a carver. This is unlike the bigger African elephants, which usually grow tusks, whether male or female. Also, Asian tuskers generally have correspondingly smaller tusks.

The combination of a strong Buddhist ethos, which discourages killing, and the formerly highly-developed use of the elephant for transport and work, also meant that ivory was principally taken from animals that had died of old age or disease, rather than from hunting. After all, an average price for a working animal is around US$6,000 (quoted by Lair q.v.), a substantial outlay in Thailand.

One of the few places in the country where ivory carving is still carried out is Payuhakiri District in Nakhon Sawan Province, but on a limited scale, and with nothing like the skill and attention to detail that went into this old seal. Seals were of two types: for governmental use, and those granted to individual high-ranking officials by the King. The latter were personal and known as Chaloeysak seals, examples of which were the Suriyamonthol seal and the Chantramonthol seal granted to the two Bunnag brothers. This seal is one of the former, showing a *thep,* or minor divinity, holding a lotus. Five cm (2 in) in diameter, it is carved slightly convex, for rolling firmly onto the paper.

As became the custom for official seals, it is shaped in the form of a *chedi,* Thai for stupa, or a reliquary monument. The stupa, the most sacred of Buddhist buildings, derives from the solid earthen mounds in India that enshrined relics of the Buddha and became the focal points of monasteries. The detachable upper part of the seal represents the spire, composed of diminishing annulets or rings. Known in Sanskrit as *chattravali,* it originated from the royal multi-tiered parasol. This crowning of the *chedi* goes way back to the Great Stupa at Sanchi in India, begun in the 3rd century BC.

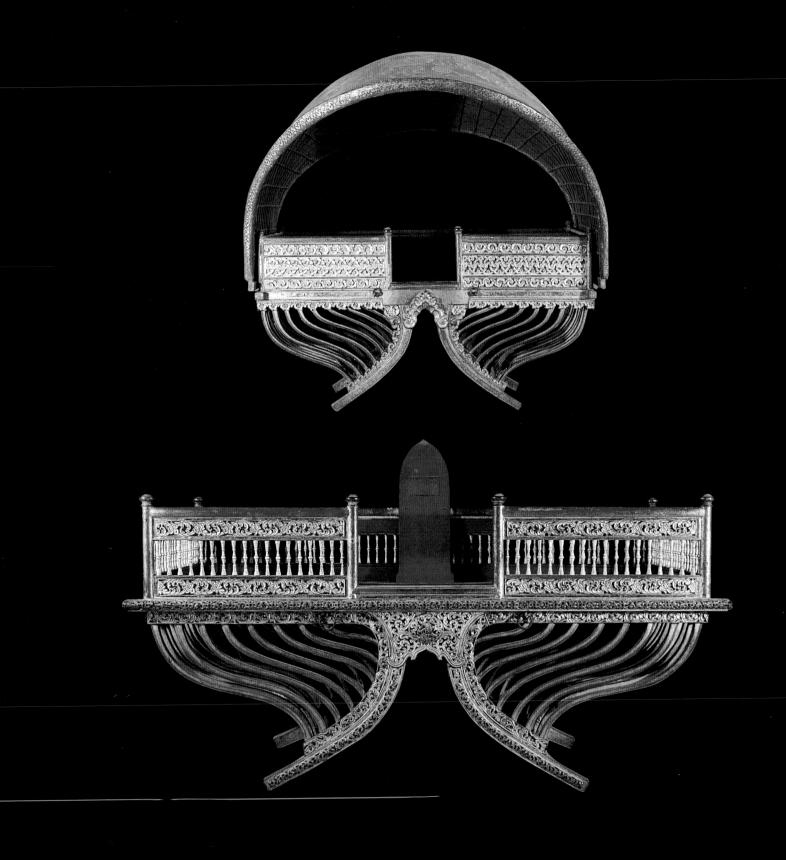

Howdahs

กูบช้าง, สัปคับ

kub chang, sapakhap

In Thailand, equipment for riding elephants evolved to some sophisticated forms, hardly surprising in a country which has used domesticated elephants for centuries. In fact, there are three times as many domesticated animals as wild in Thailand today. The Thai versions of the *howdah* (an Indian term for the seat) have a distinctive elegance. As the mural on right shows, the mahout sits on the animal's neck with his legs under the ears, the ideal 'driving' position and quite comfortable. The elephant's back is too broad to straddle, and too curved and hard to sit on comfortably.

The basic *howdah* construction is that of a wide, platform-like seat with raised sides and back, built over a yoke. It must be light but rugged, and the lower yokes need to be well turned so to fit well onto the elephant's back. *Howdahs* were made principally of wood, but the yokes were reinforced by a series of struts bent into a double-curve to provide maximum strength with the least weight. The gentle S-curve of the struts, connecting the outer side of the yoke to the underside of the platform, also helped them to act as shock absorbers as they flexed slightly with the movement of the animal. The *howdah* was tied firmly to the back of the elephant with ropes passed through rigs attached to its base and under the animal's belly.

While the basic term for the *howdah* in Thai is *yaeng chang*, there were varieties. The simplest were just seats with splayed legs and slightly raised back and sides, used by commoners and called *sapakhap*. Much more elaborate were the *howdahs* made for the nobility and for royalty. Royal *howdahs* were known as *phra thinang praphasthong* or *phra thinang lakho*, using the special term for seats or halls used by royalty. Made from valuable woods and ivory, these seats were characterized by elaborate decoration. The *howdah* shown on bottom left, now displayed in the National Museum in Chiang Mai, was used in 1926 by King Rama VII on his entry into the city of Chiang Mai—the first visit of a monarch of Siam to the North—and has detailed carving with a finish of gilded red lacquer. The seating is made from split bamboo strips.

Some of the more elegant *howdahs* were fitted with beautifully formed curved bamboo roofs, lined on the inside with cloth or paper. Favoured by noblewomen because of the protection they offered from the sun and the privacy they gave, they were referred to by a different name: *kub*. The fine gilded example shown on top left, decorated with *kanok* motifs, is in the National Museum, Lamphun.

Opposite, top: Fine gilded *howdah*, decorated with *kanok* motifs. *Opposite, bottom:* Howdah used in 1926 by King Rama VII on his entry into the city of Chiang Mai, with detailed carving and a finish of gilded red lacquer. *Above:* Mural from Nong Bua showing elephant with *mahout* and *howdah*.

Gongs

ฆ้อง

khawng

Opposite: Gong decorated in gold with characters from the Ramakien against a typical *kanok*-motif background. *Left:* Mural from Viharn Lai Kham at Wat Phra Singh in Chiang Mai depicting gong bearers in a procession. *Below:* Mural from Wat Phumin in Nan showing the circle of gongs used in traditional Thai musical ensembles (see overleaf).

Two elephant tusks support a ceremonial gong on left, in an early Rattanakosin residence. Today, this use would be frowned on, but it should be remembered that in traditional Buddhist Thailand, ivory was usually taken only from tuskers that died from natural causes.

The earliest Thai instruments were made before Indian culture made itself felt, and all had onomatopoeic names, that is, single-syllabic words that approximated the actual sound. The gong is one of these, known in Thai by the very similar-sounding *khawng.* The English word is certainly derived from the Malay *gong*; the Thai probably also. In a variety of sizes, in different combinations and put to different uses, all gongs have the same basic form: a flat front surface with a raised boss in the centre, and a thick circular rim behind, tapering slightly inwards. This rim, called *chat* after the tiered umbrella that is the symbol of royalty in Thailand, is pierced with two holes, from which the gong is suspended.

This fine example is beautifully decorated in gold with characters from the Ramakien (see pages 46–47) against a typical *kanok*-motif background. Gongs of this size, between 30 and 45 cm (12–18 in) in diameter, make a sound similar to *mong* in Thai, and so are called *khawng mong.* One of the several original

uses of such gongs was recording the passage of hours, as bells were rung in Europe. In Thailand, however, two different instruments were used: a drum for the night hours and a gong for the day. A legacy of this is the vocabulary in modern Thai for the time of day. Daylight hours, beginning at 7 o'clock, use the word for gong in conjunction with the hour, as in *sawng mong chao*, meaning 'second morning hour', or 8 o'clock. The 'thum' sound of the drum yielded the expression for evening hours, so 8 pm is *sawng mong thum.* The word for an hour is *chua mong*—literally the interval of time between the soundings of the gong.

Gongs of different sizes had many ritual uses, as in processions (see top), and are still used in some ceremonies. They were also an important percussion instrument in the Thai musical ensemble, the *piphat.* Groupings varied from a pair (one high-toned, the other low-toned) suspended in a small wooden box open at the top, to the circle of gongs, as in the mural painting on right. The player sits inside the circle with a beater in each hand, the gongs arranged clockwise in ascending pitch: the smallest at the far left, behind the player, to the largest at the far right and behind. Considerable dexterity and suppleness is needed to play them.

Musical instruments

เครื่องดนตรีไทย

kreung dontri thai

Above: Lacquered panel showing court musicians playing stringed instruments and percussion. *Opposite:* A type of stringed instrument known as the *saw duang,* a two-stringed instrument. *Opposite, far right:* Musician playing the *saw sam sai,* a three-stringed instrument.

Classical Thai music is, to Western ears, rather difficult—not always melodious, often plaintive, as if in a minor key. This is largely because the scale is divided in seven equal intervals, which ensures that the chromatic scale is impossible. The English composer Sir Herbert Parry (who wrote the music for the hymn 'Jerusalem') found that "not a single note between a starting note and its octave agrees with any notes of the European scale". Or, as a modern writer put it, the notes "fall between the cracks of the piano keyboard". Its distinctive sound reflects the independence and sense of identity of Thai culture as a whole.

Not surprisingly, classical music is produced by instruments unique to the region, and some unique to Thailand. There are, in fact, more than 50 Thai musical instruments, including regional varieties, and they are all fitted to do one thing and one thing only, which is to play Thai music. There are two principal orchestral ensembles, which date from at least the middle of the 14th century, the Sukhothai period. As noted on the previous spread, the *phiphat,* which is most commonly heard nowadays accompanying Thai kick-boxing matches, is a tuned percussion ensemble, the centrepiece being a circle of gongs within which the player sits, handling the basic

melody. The *mahori* is an ensemble that includes stringed instruments, and it is this that stretches the appreciation of those listeners unfamiliar with the form.

The large stringed instrument lying flat on the floor, where it is played, is the *chakae,* named for its fancied resemblance to a crocodile. The player depresses the strings over the frets with one hand while plucking them, usually with an ivory plectrum, with the other. The other instrument shown here is the *saw,* a kind of viol (the generic stringed instrument played with a bow, as in violin, viola and violoncello—abbreviated to cello). In sound, however, little else compares. The *saw* has been a part of the Thai orchestral ensemble since at least the middle of the 14th century, the Sukhothai period. Old texts, including the 'Traiphum Phra Ruang' and court regulations, mention it as a highly regarded instrument, ideal for accompanying singing because of its ability to blend with the human voice, but difficult to master. The version in the main picture on right is the *saw duang,* with just two strings. The resonance box is made from hardwood, covered at one end with snakeskin (python or boa constrictor), the other end left open, and its resemblance to a kind of snare used for trapping edible lizards in the North,

called a *duang dak yae*, gives this variety of *saw* its name. The tone is high and penetrating, and not at all easy for a Western listener.

Another type of *saw*, being played in the picture on far right, is the saw *sam sai*, the 'three-stringed sa', distinctive for its rounded triangular body above a spiked leg. In fact, the shape of the box is due to the unusual variety of coconut shell from which it is made. King Rama II, who ruled from 1809 to 1824, had a passion for this instrument, which he played with great skill, and apparently decreed that any owner of a coconut tree which produced this rare shape would be exempt from taxes.

One famous piece for the *saw*, known as 'The Song of the Floating Moon' or 'The Song of the Royal Dream', was composed by the King after he had heard it in a dream. He taught it to the court musicians, and it has been handed down from player to player ever since. This indeed is how classical Thai music has developed and been maintained over the centuries. There is no notation; everything is memorized and passed on by tradition.

Khon masks

หัวโขน
hua khon

Masked dance drama is at the heart of Thai theatrical tradition, accompanied by an orchestra and chorus. It derives from Indian ritual temple dancing, and is believed to have originated from the south of the country, in Nakhon Si Thammarat, which had early contacts with Indian culture, and from there spread to Sukhothai and to Cambodia.

There is no evidence remaining of its actual performance at Sukhothai, but in Ayutthaya, masked dance drama was certainly a royal entertainment and performed in the halls and courts of the palace by torchlight, without scenery. Because the dance was considered too athletic and strenuous for women, men played both male and female roles, and the complex narrative was aided by a set of masks which identified each character.

These masks—*khon* in Thai—were of great importance in establishing the character, and became an art form in their own right. Master craftsmen were responsible for some famous examples: their forms and styles were decreed both in old manuscripts and by information handed down from master to apprentice. The masks are made of papier-maché over a terracotta mould, using the thin bark from the native *khoi* tree, which is stripped, soaked in water and beaten with a mallet to separate the fibres. The *khoi* paper is pressed sheet by sheet over the mould, using rice-flour paste. Some 15 layers are needed, and when dry the mask is removed from the mould by making two long incisions down each side and the two halves peeled away. They are then re-combined, with more paper to cover the joins. Details are

added with lacquer that is heated until it can be worked into cords that are pressed onto the masks to form ridges, and with ornaments of cow-hide and mother-of-pearl. Paint and gold leaf complete the decoration.

The masks shown here, a small selection from a complete set, are miniatures, for the art of mask-making attracted its own aficionados, for whom miniature sets were made. The story line for all *khon* performances was the Thai version of the ancient Indian epic romance, the Ramayana, a moral tale of good and evil, and of the duties of kingship, and even the sacred legitimacy of kingship—this last feature made it particularly popular with rulers. The hero is Rama (third from left), an incarnation of the god Vishnu, and in the Thai version, known as the Ramakien, he is called Phra Ram. He is

usually painted deep green, usually wearing a slight smile, signifying his benevolent nature, and a multi-tiered gold crown. His purpose in the Ramakien is to defeat the demons, who threaten the gods' power.

His mortal enemy, who near the beginning of the story abducts Phra Ram's beautiful wife Nang Sida, is the evil King Thotsakan (fifth from left), ruler of Langka (the island of Sri Lanka). Thotsakan's mask, as befits his wicked nature, is demonic, with miniature demon faces on his crown. Phra Ram's ally in the quest to rescue Nang Sida is the monkey general Hanuman (second from left), son of the wind god and totally devoted to Phra Ram. He is always the great favourite of audiences, and the most highly regarded part by actors because of his acrobatic performances. Hanu-

man's mask is white, and ornamented to suit his description as having "diamond hair and crystal fangs".

The gold mask with the more human features (far left) is that of the Rusi (taken from the Sanskrit *rishi*, a holy man), and the mask itself is credited with special powers. Because of its spiritual power, this mask when used in performance is kept apart and treated votively before each *Khon* performance, which it must bless.

Khon performances are rarely staged nowadays. The full Ramakien, in 138 episodes and with 311 characters, took a staggering 720 hours, and even shortened versions used to take more than 20 hours, and were staged over two long nights. The complexity and length became too much for modern audiences. The masks, however, endure.

From left to right: Miniature *khon* masks depicting key characters in the masked dance drama: hermit, Hanuman, Phra Ram, Phra Prom, Thotsakan, Nilapat, Seng-Athit and Pipek. *Above:* Close-up view of the demon ruler Sattasoon.

Dancer's nail extenders

เล็บโนรา

lep norah

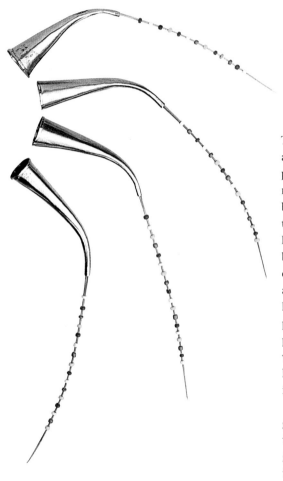

Thai dance depends heavily on gesture. Great attention is paid in the training process to producing graceful limb positions. In turn, this requires considerable suppleness, which must be learnt from an early age. In the past, dance training was a normal part of education. An English author, W. A. Graham, wrote at the beginning of the 20th century that "children of both sexes, but more especially the females, are instructed in the art, and though their limbs may not acquire the extraordinary suppleness and double-jointedness which enable professionals to bend their elbows the wrong way and to turn their fingers back over the hand to touch the wrist, yet some proficiency is usually attained".

To further accentuate these extreme hand gestures, nail extenders were invented, moulded to carry the natural curve of the dancer's fingers even further. In fact, regional versions of these metal 'nails' were developed to accompany the regional styles of dance. The extenders shown here are among the least well-known, from the South, and are used by dancers who act out *norah* performances, a traditional routine of song and dance that is unique to the area.

Formerly, prized nail extenders were made of silver and even gold, but the ones shown here are composed of thin stainless steel—

affordable enough to help maintain the dance tradition which, although still taught in many local schools, is at some risk of dying out. Thummanit Nikomrat, lecturer at the Rajabhat Institute in Songkhla, fears that the art of making the nails is rapidly being lost: "Apart from the precise techniques for designing the nails, the local artisans must have knowledge of the *norah* performance as well as the dancers' hand movements so they can use proper material. And the nail can last for eight to ten years."

One of the best of these craftsmen is Lung Kun Suwannarat, who made the set shown here and works in a village near Songkhla. He explains the process: "The most difficult step is to cut the stainless steel sheet into the triangle-like piece and then smooth its edges. After that, it is bent into the conical form." Into the tip is inserted a long thin strip of wild rattan, known locally as *hwai pon*, no more than half a centimetre (0.3 in) in diameter, and over this are pushed more than a dozen beads, carefully separated along its length. "The rattan must be bent in harmony with the curve of the stainless steel nail," adds Lung Kun. On average Lung Kun makes 86 nails a day, but it takes between five and ten days to complete each order. A set consists of just eight nails (none are worn

on the thumbs), and the sizes vary to suit the age of the dancer, who is typically between eight and ten years old. Remarkably, the price is the equivalent of four US dollars.

The fluidity and speed of the hand movements in *norah* dance make it essential that the nails fit perfectly, hence the different sizes made. Traditionally, the dancer, who would attach the nails last of all, after donning 14 pieces of costume, would lick each finger before inserting it in the metal nail. The combination of saliva and a vacuum was usually sufficient, but as the performance went on, the nails would lose their vacuum, and dancers would occasionally pause to lick and re-stick their nail. "That was a common scene on stage," said Kun Lung, himself a devotee of the performances. The modern solution, less elegant in close-up but allowing for an uninterrupted dance, is to use adhesive tape.

Left and right: Set of stainless steel nail extenders made by Lung Kun Suwannarat, a skilled craftsman based in a village close to Songkhla. *Above:* Dancer illustrating how nail extenders accentuate the graceful repertoire of hand movements characteristic of Thai classical dance.

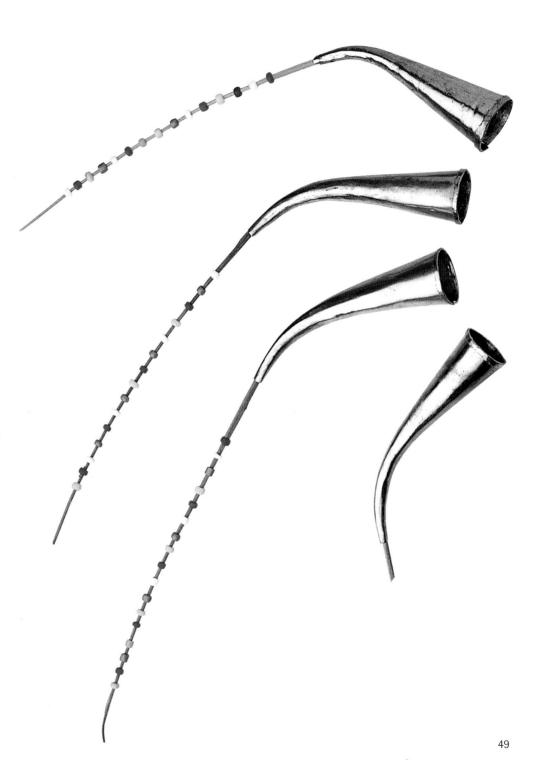

Floral decorations and
fruit and vegetable carvings
การจัดดอกไม้, ผักและผลไม้แกะสลัก
karn chud dok mai, pak lae polamai kae salak

The Thai decorative sensibility, highly developed in such fields as furniture, lacquerware, ceramics and so on, also receives expression in less likely places—food and flowers. Both of these artforms were developed at the royal court, and the ephemeral nature of the materials enhances their intricate beauty. Indeed, both have a continuing royal use, and some of the finest output is produced at the Grand Palace in Bangkok. There is a hereditary post of fruit and vegetable carver, with premises at the Palace, while almost every day garlands and floral compositions are created by a team of women working in the Inner Court.

The carving of fruit and vegetables evolved as part of the elaborate ritual of royal Thai cuisine. While the daintification of flavour is not to everyone's taste, the refinement of appearance has been developed into a distinctive decorative art. A key feature of this is imitation—carving fruits and vegetables into what they are not, such as carrots into roses, papayas into chrysanthemums and cucumbers into leaves.

Special tiny paring knives are made for this purpose, but all professional carvers then further grind and hone the blades into idiosyncratic shapes, some like miniature sickles. The design repertoire is similar to the

floral motifs used in carving and gilded lacquer, and a variety of special techniques have been invented. For example, a fresh chilli can be turned into a flower in the following way. With the chilli held horizontally by the base, the thin sharp point of the knife is inserted close to the base and drawn back to the tip. The chilli is then rotated 90 degrees and sliced in the same way. This produces four slivers, still attached to the base, and by rotating the chilli by 45 degrees then 90 degrees, eight slivers are created. The chilli is then de-seeded and dropped into iced water, upon which the slivers curl back elegantly into petals.

Carving techniques on larger vegetables and fruits involve a complex series of incisions from which thin wedges are removed. The best effects are achieved when there is a marked colour contrast between the pulp and the rind or skin, as in a cucumber (pale green to dark striped green) and water-melon (red to green).

Floral compositions demand the same painstaking intricacy, and a good place to see them is the all-day-and-night flower market of Pak Klong Dalat in Bangkok, a little south of the Grand Palace and Wat Po. Most are used as offerings of one kind or another, and the most common is the *malai* (garland), with white jasmine and yellow marigold as key components.

Opposite: Close-up picture of the skilled art of vegetable carving. *Top:* A *malai* or garland made from jasmine. *Middle:* Orchids deftly stringed as decoration. *Above:* Flower and leaf designs are popular vegetable carvings.

Traditional Thai costumes

ชุดไทย
chud thai

Above: Traditional costume seen on the rowers of the Royal Barge. *Opposite:* Formal occasions such as at the Ploughing Ceremony are when Thai traditional costume is often worn as a source of national pride. *Far right:* Thai dancers in traditional costume.

National dress is a rarity in most countries, reserved, if at all, for special ceremonies and occasions. The onslaught of Western style in so many things has proved irresistible to most cultures, and costume has accompanied the material benefits that the West exported throughout much of the 20th century. Thailand is no exception, succumbing in particular to a deliberate Westernization during the post-war Phibun administration.

Nevertheless, national dress in its various forms puts in more frequent appearances in Thailand than it does elsewhere, due largely to a resurgence of interest in traditional costume and fabrics during the reign of the present monarch. Her Majesty Queen Sirikit prefers to wear Thai classical costume for ceremonial occasions, and this has encouraged not only court use, but dressing traditionally at all formal occasions. There are now modern interpretations of ancient styles, with names such as Thai Reuan Ton, Thai Chakri, Thai Boromphimarn, Thai Dusit, and Thai Chitlada. There is both an element of national pride in this, and a celebration of the now fully revived and very successful Thai fabric industry (see pages 30–31 for the story behind Thai silk).

In fact, as you can see from the several mural paintings elsewhere in this book,

traditional Thai dress varies across both social classes and regionally, and the most wide-spread item is the tube-skirt (see pages 136–7). The classical costumes, however, are derived from the court during different periods of Thai history. As this history has involved considerable influence from neighbouring peoples such as the Khmer, Lao, Burmese, Malays and even Indonesians, it is not surprising that the costumes themselves are related.

It was, however, the Sukhothai period that saw the emergence of a distinctive Siamese style, and it was at this time, in the 14th and 15th centuries, that one of the items most indicative of a national costume was develoed —the *chong kraban*, a kind of skirt in which the cloth is gathered together and threaded between the legs, over three-quarter-length pants. The *chong kraban* seems to have been influenced by the *yak rung* worn by the Khmer, but it is now firmly embedded in Thai costume.

The *chong kraban* persisted into the Ayutthayan period, although women more often wore a tube-skirt with front-pleated lengths of cloth. At the top of the body, they wore a long-sleeved blouse and draped a *sabai* over one shoulder (see pages 140–1). The dress of royalty and aristocracy became ever more elaborate, embellished with jewellery and

several designs of tiered crown. Such formal dress only occasionally appears now, but an echo of it can still be seen in the costumes worn by temple dancers.

There is an additional tradition to do with colour—which is appropriate to the time and the occasion. In a poem entitled 'Sawatdiruksa', the Ayutthayan poet Sunthornphu mentions that red should be worn on Sunday, white on Monday, violet and dark indigo on Tuesday, bright orange on Wednesday, green and yellow on Thursday, gray like the colour of a rain cloud on Friday and black on Saturday. These colours were favourable both for daily wear and—a sign of those historical times—when going to war!

Religious Paraphernalia

Objects made in the service of Buddhism

In many instances no less sumptuous than the items produced for royalty and the nobility, religious art in Thailand formed the foundation of all secular art, architecture and decoration. Theravada Buddhism, the tr aditional and to its adherents the pure form of Buddhism, inspired a form of art that was much more restricted in its focus of devotion than the more eclectic Mahayana cult that spread north to Tibet, China, Korea and Japan. Nevertheless, given the Thai passion for decorative art, the ornament lavished on sacred architecture, icons and paraphernalia was as rich as each community could afford—be it in a village, town or palace.

Buddha images

พระพุทธรูป
phra puttha roop

Whatever recent modernization Thailand appears to have gone through, Buddhism still underpins daily life and culture. Images of the Buddha still play an important and complex role. Every one of the 30,000 or so monasteries in the country has a principal image, often of considerable size, and many have in addition a number of smaller statues. Any devout household also maintains its own altar with at least one statue, and if the owners are of some means, there may be a special room set aside for the image, like a private chapel. In size, images range from the gigantic (the seated Phra Achana statue at Wat Si Chum in Sukhothai is 14.7 m [48.2 ft] in height) to the minuscule (personal images as small as a centimeter [0.4 in]).

Every image is considered a substitute for the Buddha (as is the abbot of a monastery), and in some sense is believed to have life. Thais pay respect to Buddha images in a particular way, touching their forehead to the floor three times. In doing this, they are honouring first the Buddha, then the doctrine, and finally the monkhood—the so-called 'Triple Gem'. In essence, each one of these three represents the others; they are interlinked.

One reason for the proliferation of Buddha images is that the act of commissioning or donating one is considered meritorious. According to Buddhism, every action has a result, so good deeds increase one's store of merit. In the North, from about the 16th century, it became common to inscribe the bases of images, often with the name of the donors. Human nature being what it is, this practise is a short step away from offering an image in return for a specific wish—and most of the smaller images are votive.

Buddha images are made in many different materials and styles. The medium used varies according to what is available and the skills of the sculptor or craftsman. Pride of place is given to bronze casting, a skill for which Thailand has been famous since the 14th century. However, many other materials are used. For example, the small green image pictured overleaf is of Siberian jade on a ruby base and was made by Fabergé, who took commissions from the Thai court in the 19th century.

Thai Buddha images cover a considerable—even bewildering—variety of styles, drawing influences over the course of history from all the surrounding Buddhist nations. Every so often, a direct injection of ideals was received from Sri Lanka which, once the religion had declined in its native India, became the source of the canon. Crucial to an appreciation of

Left: A very fine Buddha head, from the National Museum in Bangkok. *Below:* A small green image from a private collection. Carved from Siberian jade on a ruby base, it was made by Fabergé, who took commissions from the Thai court in the 19th century. *Far right:* Bronze walking Sukhothai-style Buddha from Wat Benjamabopit, Bangkok.

Buddhist art is the set of rules, the iconography, for portraying the Buddha. There is simply not the scope for artistic interpretation that exists in, say, Christian art. In particular, there are 32 major and 80 minor distinguishing features which set the Buddha apart from ordinary men, and which emphasize his other-worldliness. Some are quite strange, if not anatomically impossible, such as a nose like a parrot's beak, a chin like a mango stone, arms like the trunk of an elephant, projecting heels, and webbed hands and feet. Nevertheless, if the image is to serve its purpose, it must go some way in conforming to these ideals.

Beyond this, there are endless diversions into the ideals of proportion; endless arguments, too. One Thai manuscript categorizes three types: 'banyan', 'elephant', and 'lion' characteristics. Another specifies that the nose should not be in alignment with the chest, but with the palm instead, and that in a standing image the body should be seven times the length of the face. These are all prescriptions for an image that appears 'calm and beautiful'.

The peak of Thai Buddhist art was during the Sukhothai period of the 14th and 15th centuries. It coincided with stronger attempts to convey these ideals—and resulted in representations of the Buddha that are

ethereal, other-worldly and asexual. Exactly how this came about is unknown, but at some point in the 14th century, a radically different style evolved. The face is elongated into an ovoid and its features are conveyed in a set of elegant, sinuous curves: high arched eyebrow ridges lead down to the ridge of the nose and are echoed in the triple curve of the eyelids and mouth. There is a purity and a tension in these curves that led scholar and collector Alexander Griswold to describe the Sukhothai style as "full of nervous energy", a remarkable achievement given that the figure also exudes calm and peace.

And within this unique Sukhothai style, one invention stands clear, that of the walking Buddha. It appears nowhere else, and relates to the placing of his imprint—a symbol, important throughout Southeast Asia, of the spread of the religion. In particular, it refers to the Buddha pacing to and fro in the third week after his enlightenment at Bodhgaya. The magic created by the Sukhothai sculptors has produced a free-standing image with a flowing, almost supernatural, sinuosity. Among the many examples, the famous bronze figure at Wat Benjamabopit, Bangkok, shown on right, is generally considered to be the finest.

Buddha's hands

ปาง

pang

Left: Gilded wooden hand in *abhaya mudra* with the palm up turned. *Right:* Close-up of Buddha hand in *bhumisparsa mudra*, where the right hand is resting on the right knee and the fingers just touch the ground. From Wat Si Chum in Sukhothai. *Far right:* Standing Buddha with hand in *abhaya mudra* from Wat Saphan Hin, Sukhothai.

Of particular eloquence is the gesture of the hand of the Buddha, the 'mudra' in Sanskrit. Indeed, this alone can represent the entire Buddha image, and it is not uncommon to see isolated hands, as for practical reasons they were carved or cast separately from the main body, and so not infrequently become detached. The *mudras* are symbolic movements and positions of the hand that were originally used by monks in meditation and other spiritual exercises as a way of creating spiritual energy. There are about half a dozen commonly used in Thailand, and all refer back to an incident in the life of the historical Buddha. Nowadays, however, the *mudras* are restricted to Buddha images, and in Thailand two of them are seen much more often than any other.

They are the *abhaya mudra* for dispelling fear and the *bhumisparsa mudra* of calling the earth to witness. In the picture on left, the gilded wooden upturned palm is in *abhaya mudra*—nearly always made with the right hand, occasionally with both, and on standing or walking Buddhas. The Phra Attharat Buddha shown on far right—standing 12.5 m (41 ft) tall amid the ruins of Wat Saphan Hin on a ridge overlooking Sukhothai—uses this gesture. It refers to the occasion when the Buddha's cousin, Devadatta, full of envy at the greatness and

success of the Enlightened One, sent a ferocious elephant, a known man-killer, to attack him. As the elephant, called Nalagiri, charged and all the disciples fled except Ananda, the Buddha raised his hand, and with the strength of his compassion, calmed the animal and stroked its trunk. He said: "Do not approach the Buddha, elephant, with the idea of harming him, for that will cause you suffering. A killer of the Buddha will find no good state either here or after death."

Even more widely represented is the gesture of the seated Buddha known as *bhumisparsa mudra*, in which the right hand rests on the right knee (the Buddha being seated in lotus position) and the fingertips just touching the ground. It refers to a pivotal moment in the Enlightenment. Gautama the man, on the verge of Buddhahood, seated himself cross-legged under a great pipal tree and resolved to achieve full understanding of the cessation of suffering (the key to Enlightenment), saying: "I shall not change this my position so long as I have not done what I set out to do."

With success in sight, the future Buddha was cajoled and finally attacked by Mara, the Tempter, and his demons, using thunderbolts. However, the Buddha dispersed the army of temptations with love, compassion and wisdom.

Addressing Mara, he proclaimed his victory, adding: "There is no need for a witness. This very earth is my witness." At this, he stretched his right hand to the ground, which shook, scattering the cohorts of Mara. The earth-touching hand shown on left is the height of a man, and belongs to the colossal seated Buddha at Wat Si Chum at Sukhothai.

Votive tablets

พระพิมพ์

phra pim

When the ancient capital at Sukhothai was being excavated by archaeologists (and unfortunately also by illegal treasure hunters), large numbers of small tablets were found buried. Most were of baked or unbaked clay, a few in silver, gold or pewter, all carrying images of the Buddha. They were portable Buddhist icons, and Sukhothai is not the only place where they have been found. They were buried in the most sacred parts of many temple complexes, in caves used for meditation, and inside stupas.

The three pictured here are by no means typical. They are from Sukhothai, and each has exceptional qualities. The gilded clay tablet (on right), from the Chao Sam Phraya Museum in Ayutthaya, features an interpretation of the famous walking Buddha (see page 59) that is unusually finely worked for its size. The silver votive tablet (on left), also from the Chao Sam Phraya Museum and manufactured by the *repoussée* techniques, shows the Buddha in the most widely used of all postures in Thailand, *bhumisparsa*, touching the earth with his right hand upon achieving Enlightenment (see page 61). Less usually, the sacred bodhi tree under which he is seated is depicted in realistic detail. The third votive piece (far right), in near-perfect condition, is in gold *repoussée*,

21 cm (8 in) high and found at Wat Phra Pai Luang, also in Sukhothai. In the U-Thong style, from the 15th–16th centuries, it shows a stance unique to Sukhothai and its dependants, with the arms held straight down at the sides. This is popularly known as *phra poet lok* in Thai, literally 'Buddha opening the world(s)', and refers to the Buddha's descent from the Trayastrimsa heaven, when he opened the three worlds of heaven, earth and hell, so that all beings could see each other.

One of the most interesting aspects of votive tablets is how they developed from being devotional Buddhist objects into the modern cult of amulets (see pages 64–65). The distinction between the two is not completely clear either, as it is claimed that many amulets sold on the market now are ancient votive tablets. Moreover, while it is difficult to be sure to what use these old votive tablets were put at the time they were made, it is known that many were carried home by early pilgrims visiting sacred sites. In one sense, they could be considered the earliest tourist souvenirs, though within a sacred context.

The practice originated in India. In her book, *Votive Tablets in Thailand* (1997), M. L. Pattaratorn Chirapravati notes that Chinese monks who visited India in the second

century wrote accounts that described the stamping of tablets. Using press moulds, monks made these tablets not only for distribution among the faithful, but also as a meditative exercise.

While souvenirs of a type, votive tablets were—and still are—considered intrinsically sacred. One practice that was followed, particularly in the south of Thailand, was for the powder from the cremated remains of senior monks and revered religious teachers to be ground up into the clay used for stamping. This undoubtedly contributed to the more recent amulet cult, and fostered the belief that such tablets would contain special powers.

Amulets

พระเครื่อง
phra kreung

Votive tablets (see pages 62-63) began as sacred mementoes of visits to holy places, but over time went through a process of change, acquiring, in the minds of believers, the ability to protect. In the streets around Wat Mahathat in Bangkok, close to the Grand Palace, pavement stalls sell amulets, which are essentially votive Buddhist tablets to which are ascribed specific powers. More than this, some half a dozen Thai collectors' magazines, and even a dealer's website, specialize in amulets. Amulet collection in Thailand is now a significant business, with the rarest items changing hands for more than a million baht apiece.

It was during the reign of King Rama V, towards the end of the 19th century, that votive tablets began to be treated in significant numbers as amulets. However, there is some evidence that the cult began in the reign of his father, King Mongkut (Rama IV). It is likely that one catalyst was the new popularity of collecting antiques that spread from the court, and because of increasing demand, ancient sites began to be excavated illegally. At first, the clay votive tablets were held in little regard, but gradually their provenance, and the idea that the monks who had created them must have transferred into them some of their power, made them increasingly desirable.

By the early 20th century, the cult had become established, although its relatively rapid development is clear from the comments of King Rama VI, who ruled from 1910 to 1925, and wrote: "It is astounding that people hang votive tablets around the necks as self-protection." Today, most Thai men across all classes carry an amulet; women to a lesser extent.

To a casual non-Thai observer, such an amulet may appear to lack refinement, workmanship, even distinctiveness. However, two essential qualities are hidden: the person who made it, and its composition. Most amulets are of clay, but this medium is often very complex, being mixed with a number of unusual ingredients which contribute to its power, including certain seeds, dried flowers, herbs, pollen, and the ash of burnt sacred texts. Moreover, if the composition was made by a revered senior monk, it will benefit from his power.

Two examples of dealers' notes give some flavour of the arcane qualities that amulet-collectors seek. They describe two of the most famous amulets, Phra Somdej (the name of a famous old monk), and the strange Phra Pid Ta ('Buddha with Eyes Closed'):

"There are only five forms of Somdej Wat Rakang: Make sure you have seen a genuine one before and compare it with other Phra Pim Somdej to spot the differences. Look at the texture and the substance and examine the composition, which has been moulded out of burnt limestone and then mixed with Chinese Tung oil and holy matters such as Med Chad, Med Phradhati, Holy Dried Flower, Dried Stream Rice etc."

"Luang Phor Thub (Designated Name is Phra Kru Dhebsit-dhepa-dhibbodi) is the ninth in order of former Chief Abbot of the Wat, who has created the most revered Phra Pid-Ta and Pid-Dhavarn of Wat Thong in the year BE 2442 (AD 1899). Amulets were created between the years BE 2442 to 2453; the major proportion were Phra Pid-Dhavarn: nine human orifices' closed gesture, and the minor proportion were Phra Pid-Ta: eyes closed gesture."

With rare, sought-after amulets commanding prices in excess of US$20,000, many fakes abound, but even this is not straightforward. Reproductions of famous, costly amulets are common, yet once they have been sanctified by a monk, they will still afford protection to the owner—as long as he or she respects it, and behaves well, according to Buddhist precepts.

Ceramic propitiatory figurines

ตุ๊กตา
tukata

Located at one end of the courtyard of Wat Ratchanaddaram, across the canal from Bangkok's prominent Golden Mount, is a small market devoted to amulets and other votive paraphernalia. There are rows of tiny, mass-produced, doll-like figures, such as Chinese goddesses, white-bearded sages, King Rama V, fat laughing Buddhas, children with ancient costumes and hair arranged in the traditional top-knot (at top), and strange creatures with bodies of men and heads of a variety of animals.

Despite their gaudy aspect and the cheap material used, the figurines are not toys but propitiatory offerings placed at shrines, spirit houses (see overleaf) and temples. The ceramic kilns at Sukhothai and Si Satchanalai (see page 17) fired thousands of similar figurines in the 14th to 15th centuries; the glazed examples below are typical. The colours varied from white to celadon to brown, and black under-painting was occasionally used to emphasize details, as in the man on a bull at below, far left (Sangkhalok ceramic, Ramkamhaeng).

What makes these individually modelled pieces so much more interesting than the mould-stamped modern versions is the love and observation that clearly has been put into them. None are masterpieces, but the work of local craftsmen who draw on their own experience and the life around them to create spontaneous as well as sincere works. The mother-and-child figure, definitely mass-produced from the quantities that have been unearthed, was a particular favourite, and usually lovingly observed. In the woman-and-

Spirit houses

ศาลพระภูมิ

san phra phum

Animism runs deep in Thai belief, although without conflicting with Buddhism. Traditional belief systems revolve around the hierarchy of spirits, or *phi*. The spirits who have unlocalized, general dominion, are broadly divided into good and harmful beings. The good, originally known as celestial spirits, or *phi fa*, later became identified as *thep*. This comes from the Indian *devata*, meaning minor divinities, and often inaccurately translated into English as 'angels' (as in 'City of Angels', the Thai name for Bangkok, Krung Thep).

Of most immediate importance to daily life, however, are the territorial spirits, who live with nature and are identified with its physical elements, such as water, mountains, caves and forests. They are not only spirits of place but also masters—*jao*—of their particular area of the natural environment. As such, they must be propitiated so that they will not be offended by the humans who must share the habitat with them. More than that, the spirits' help is needed to assure success for the family and the community.

There are in total nine territorial guardian spirits. These are: Protector of the House; Protector of the Gates and Stairways; Protector of the Bridal Chamber; Protector of the Animals; Protector of the Store-houses and Barns; Protector of the Fields and Paddies; Protector of the Orchards and Gardens; Protector of the Terraces; and Protector of the Temples and Religious Establishments.

Traditionally, temporary shrines were erected for ceremonial occasions when the spirits had to be invoked: birth, marriage, death and housebuilding. This practice at housebuilding led to the maintenance of a permanent shrine, because there was always the risk that the guardian spirit of the land, *phra phum*, would not accept the continued presence of the householder and his family. They were, after all, usurping the spirit by erecting a building and moving in. The full title of the guardian spirit is *phra phum jao thi*, the final two words meaning 'master of the place'. A specialist is needed to supervise the siting of the spirit house, to make sure that every aspect is appropriate. If, for instance, it were located in the shadow of the house, the spirit would not give his protection. Daily offerings of a little rice are placed at the spirit house, and a special annual offering of pig's head and chicken is given, usually on New Year's Day (this occurs in April in Thailand).

The spirit house generally takes the form of a miniature traditional Thai house, usually with a little porch or veranda on which the offerings are placed. The style is open to interpretation, as these examples show. Figurines, as we saw on the previous pages, are often placed within the tiny house. One specific figure is Jawet, a divinity holding a sword, or a book and whip. The book contains the register of the good and evil acts committed by humans living within the area.

In village communities, the guardian spirit of the land is honoured as the *phra phum ban* (spirit of the village) with a specific (quite substantial) shrine in the form of a small house raised on posts, and located in its own fenced enclosure. Every year, at a special ceremony, the community traditionally offers food and other gifts. This custom is still maintained to an extent, but in the past it was taken very seriously. A British engineer, Holt Hallett, recounts, in his book *A Thousand Miles on an Elephant in the Shan States* (1988), that when he was there in 1976, the villages were closed off and "forbidden to strangers on the occasion of the sacrifice to the village tutelary spirit at the new year".

Opposite: Placing offerings at the spirit house is a daily occurence. *Above:* Spirit houses often mimic the architecture of the houses they are protecting.

Offering receptacles

ขันโตก

khan dok, phan waen fah

Offerings play a large part in Thai religious life, and are the focus of much of the daily inter-action between a monastery and the lay community. This relationship is at its clearest and most traditional in rural Thailand, where it is unobscured by the overlay of urbanization in the cities and large towns. It differs from, say, the relationship between a Christian church, or a Jewish synagogue, and its respective congregations in a number of ways. There are parallels, such as the preaching of sermons, prayer and the role of members of the religious order in conducting ceremonies of rites of passage, such as birth, marriage and death, but there are some very distinct differences, of which at least two influence the presentation of offerings.

One major distinction between the Thai *wat* and most religious buildings outside Buddhism is that the *wat* functions as a monastery. Even this needs qualification, because to most Westerners the word is most likely to conjure up the picture of a secluded community of monks who have withdrawn from the world for a lifetime, perhaps even having taken vows, such as of silence. This is not the case in the more than 30,000 *wat* in Thailand, because of the nature of the kind of Buddhism practised.

At an early stage in its development, possibly in the first century AD, Buddhism split into two doctrines. The break-away form, which went on to establish itself in Tibet, China, Korea and Japan (as well as in parts of South-east Asia, though not permanently), was called Mahayana, and to the world at large is probably the better known today. Its distinctive tenet is the existence of Bodhisattvas, or 'Buddhas-to-be'—beings who, on the verge of Enlightenment, delay entering Nirvana to stay and help humankind. The original doctrine, adhered to in Thailand, Sri Lanka, Burma, Laos and Cambodia, is called Theravada, the 'Doctrine of the Elders'. It emphasizes the role of the Noble Eightfold Path, the pinnacle of which is the attainment of Enlightenment.

This Path can best be followed within the discipline of monastic life, and Thai men are expected to enter the monastery for at least a short period, though not all do so. Tradition-ally, this meant that most males would spend one rainy season in their local monastery. So, the *wat* houses a community and not just one priest, and in this community, the members rotate through the *wat* and the village or town.

The influence this tradition has on offer-ings is that the religious community, which is also part of the lay community, has to be supported materially, particularly with food and clothing. In addition is the Buddhist belief that one should constantly strive to earn merit, and one very accessible way is by making religious offerings. Such offerings include practical items for the use of the monks, as well as flowers, incense and candles.

All offerings must be presented at the *wat* in a dedicated receptacle. For this purpose, there is a wide variety of offering stands, bowls and trays. The black and red Thai offertory bowl (opposite, top) is made of lacquered wood, as is the red bowl below. Of black lacquer with coloured glass inlay is the pedestal stand on the right, while the other

pedestal stand is of black and red lacquer. Most offering stands are raised, as depicted in the gilded mural from Suan Pakkaad, and they are all decorated to some degree. Some of the most common types are the stands for carrying flowers, known as *khan dok* or, if triangular, *khan kaeo thang sam*. Another stand, a two-tiered receptacle called the *phan waen fa* is used for the annual presentation of robes at the Kathin ceremony, while trays with covers, like the *tieb* on page 15, are used to hold food.

71

Left and Opposite, middle: Red and black lacquered bamboo alms bowl, made as an offering for a high-ranking monk. *Far right:* Every morning before dawn monks process through the vicinity of their monasteries collecting their daily food. The monks at top receiving rice offerings at Wat Hari Punchai, while the novices from the same monastery below line up for alms. They all carry the standard black lacquered bowls.

Alms bowls

บาตร
batr

Each day before dawn, in every village and town throughout Thailand, barefoot monks leave their monastery precincts, in twos and threes from the smaller monasteries, or in long lines from the larger ones. The monks walk in silence along the side of roads, and, at houses and shops where they expect food to be offered, stop and turn to face the entrance. Someone typically hurries out with a basin of rice and a scoop. The monks remove the lid from their alms bowl—an almost spherical bowl—and receive the offering with both hands, still in silence. Should no one appear, they wait a few seconds before moving on. In making this daily round, the monks are continuing the tradition of the Buddha himself; in offering food, the lay community is playing its part in supporting the local monastery, and is also accruing merit in return.

At one point in his life, the Buddha visits his father, King Suthothana, before the old man dies. The last time the Buddha was in the city, he was a rich young prince, the heir to the throne, but now he is returning as the Enlightened One, shaven headed and in yellow robes; he begs for his food. The old king is shocked, and says: "Why do you want to slight me? Why do you want to beg for your food? Can't I give food to all these monks?"

"This is the practice of our lineage, O Great King," replies his son.

"Isn't our lineage the royal clan of Maha Sammatas? Not one of that lineage ever begged for food."

The Buddha gently rebukes his father: "Your lineage is that, O Great King; that is the royal lineage. Ours is the lineage of the Buddhas. All the Buddhas used to beg for their food on the road."

The practice of collecting alms—indeed, the whole idea of the renunciation of worldly values—pre-dates Buddhism. Gautama was, in many aspects of his daily life, continuing an established tradition. The Canonical texts describe how, as he renounces his luxurious life as a prince and escapes from the palace and city, an old friend takes to him "the eight requisites for a recluse: the three robes, the alms bowl, the razor, the needle, the belt and the water strainer". Even today, according to the monastic code or *Vinaya*, these are the only possessions a monk is allowed.

According to tradition, the Buddha's alms bowl was made from clay, and was simple in form. Today, alms bowls are still simple, but as they are an item appropriate for a devotee to offer to monks, people try where possible to make them fine and elegant. The beautiful

red and black lacquered bamboo alms bowl featured on left is such an offering, and it is probably meant for a high-ranking monk.

As can be observed above, the alms bowl is composed of three parts: the stand, the bowl and the lid. The novice monks, shown below at an annual festival at a large monastery in the North, Wat Hari Punchai, and the ones above, carry the standard black lacquered bowls.

Monk's fans
ตาลปัตร
talapatr

At ceremonial occasions in which Buddhist monks are in attendance, one of the more notable paraphernalia is the elaborate and decorative monk's fan. In the picture (left on facing page) we see its specific use: covering the monk's face as he delivers a sermon in Lamphun; in this particular ceremony, a group of monks arrive from the nearby monastery to bless a house, its owner and its ancestors.

Originally, monks' fans, called *talapatr* in Thai, were simpler affairs made from palm leaves, and had short handles. There are a number of theories as to their origin, one of the more practical—if not particularly delicate—being that they were for shielding the monk from the smell of putrefaction. The stench was due to the ancient custom of making monastic robes from the shroud in which a corpse has been wrapped—a symbolic act of renunciation of comfort; the monk would have to remove the cloth, using a small palm fan to cover his nose. The tradition later evolved to carrying fans to ceremonies, in particular to funerals.

Another theory is that the fan concealed the faces of monks at gatherings of the laity so that the latter could concentrate on the *dharma* being preached, rather than be distracted by the monks' appearance. A legend in Thailand concerns a disciple of the Lord Buddha, Phra Sangkachai, who was so handsome that many female members of the congregation fell in love with him. Realizing the effect that he had, Sangkajai prayed to be made unattractive. His wish was fulfilled: in certain monasteries, you will see the seated statue of a fat monk with coarse features. Thus, monks learned to hide their faces when giving sermons or officiating at ceremonies.

Beyond these tales, the Buddha himself carried a fan when he went to preach to his father, King Suthothana, and so the item has become a symbol of religious authority. It was perhaps inevitable that such a symbol would evolve from simple palm leaves into beautiful ceremonial fans, now called *pad rong.* At first, the fan was an object that ordinary people could themselves make, as an offering to monks of the local monastery. Offerings, of course, were a recognized way of acquiring merit; inscriptions found at Wat Chang Lom and dating to AD 1384 record the presentation of ceremonial fans to high-ranking monks.

Fans given as offerings began as woven bamboo or feathers, but as the greater beauty of the item would affect the degree of merit, there was continuous improvement. Carved ivory might be used, or satin, or silk, enhanced by embroidery and even gems, according to

the means and devotion of the person seeking merit. The ordinary palm-leaf fans declined in use as they appeared less and less fitting. In the detail from a painting at the Jim Thompson house (above), a monk holds his fan while he preaches to devotees.

Opposite: A painting at the Jim Thompson house depicts a monk holding a fan while preaching. *Left:* A monk delivers a sermon in Lamphun while covering his face with his fan. *Below:* Fans vary in detail and materials; what began as simple bamboo or feather fans have been replaced by more ornate affairs as seen here.

Assembly hall models

วิหารจำลอง
viharn chamlong

Highly prized because so few have survived, models of monastic buildings, in terracotta, wood and cast bronze, date mainly from the Ayutthaya period. These were not architectural models, but votive objects presented to the monastery itself. As with Buddha images, evidence from inscriptions is limited to northern Thailand, where it became fashionable to record some information on the base. In the case of the bronze model (main picture, facing page), 102 cm (40 in) tall, displayed at the Chao Sam Phraya Museum, Chiang Mai, we have a short history. It was commissioned in 1726 by a local dignitary of the town of Chiang Saen, and his wife. A model of the *viharn*, or assembly hall, of Wat Pha Khao Pan, a monastery on the banks of the Mekong River, it was cast and presented in time for the inauguration of the actual *viharn*.

Until the town's comprehensive destruction in 1804 during fierce fighting to dislodge the Burmese, Chiang Saen was an important centre, famous for its monasteries and bronze casting. Donating such a model was, as presenting a Buddha image, an act of merit. This bronze model survived the original building, which either deteriorated because of its wooden construction or, more likely, was burnt down in 1804. In any case, it is an

attractive example of northern temple architecture, which differed from that of the Central Plains. The original, however, would probably not have had such a high, tiered base: it is more likely a pedestal for the votive piece.

Most monasteries have several buildings. The most frequently used building is the *viharn*, a hall for both monks and the laity to gather in. Gabled, and with its principal entrance at one end facing east, the direction of sunrise, its interior is mainly bare save for a pulpit from which scriptures are read, and for one or more statues of the Buddha at its western end, raised on a plinth or on special tables. A second building of the same general construction is the ordination hall, called an *ubosot*, or simply *bot*. This is exclusively for the monks' use, and is sanctified by its main distinguishing feature: a set of eight markers, around its perimeter, known as *bai sema*. These halls were often the rooms that the models depicted, as seen by the two wooden models on this page: on left a *viharn* of an unknown *wat* now housed at the National Museum in Chiang Mai and above, a model of the *viharn* at Wat Theueumtong at Nan.

The terracotta model (far right), located in the Chao Sam Phraya Museum and Ayutthayan, illustrates another typical feature of traditional

MODEL OF VIHARN
LATE CHIENGSAEN STYLE 16 - 18 CENTURY A.D.

Opposite: Two wooden model assembly halls: on left a *viharn* of an unknown *wat* now housed at the National Museum in Chiang Mai and above, a model of the *viharn* at Wat Theueumtong at Nan. *Left:* Model of the *viharn* of Wat Pha Khao Pan on the banks of the Mekong River, now in the Chao Sam Phraya Museum, Chiang Mai. *Below:* Ayutthayan terracotta model, illustrating the sagging roof of Ayutthayan buildings.

Thai architecture—the sagging roof or truss. In Thai this design is called the 'underbelly of an elephant' for obvious reasons. Its populartiy ironically grew out of a structural defect of the post-and-beam construction of such buildings: the weight of the beamwork tended to compress the wood vertically. For the most part this was a problem to be corrected, but for a short period it was aesthetically appreciated.

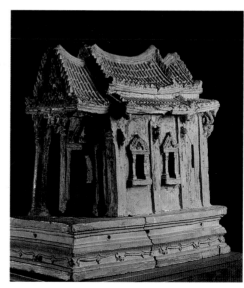

Monk's chairs

ธรรมมาสน์
thammat

Opposite: A *thammat tang* , a preaching chair with a back rest and two arm rests; the monk would sit cross-legged on this type of chair. *Right:* Type of pulpit known as a *busabok thammat*, a tiered reliquary with a tapering top for enshrining a Buddha image. *Below:* Many *thammat tang* have found their way into domestic interiors, where because of their depth a cushion is needed to support the back.

These deep, low monks' chairs, many of which have found their way into domestic interiors, have a specific function. Known as *thammat*, the chairs are intended for use by monks when preaching or reading the scriptures to a congregation. They are, in fact, just one of several designs of the ecclesiastical seat, some of which are elaborate tall structures with tiered spire roofs, others plainer and lower. All fulfil the same role as the pulpit in a church.

The Thai preaching seat has its origin at the beginning of the Sukhothai period, during the reign of King Ramkamhaeng. A 1301 inscription records that a stone throne called Phra Thaen Manangkasila-asna, which the king had built, was used by senior monks to preach from. Since then, three kinds of pulpit have evolved. The oldest, known as a *thaen* or *tiang*, and deriving from the original Sukhothai model, is a simple rectangular seat without a back rest, standing about 50 cm (20 in) high. Occasionally of stone, it is more commonly made of wood, with short legs that are often re-curved into representations of a mythical lion's paws, known as *kha singh*. This plain style is likely to be found in rural monasteries.

A second style of pulpit is the one shown right, below. The design has become popular as an item of secular furniture, not just in the West but also in some of the wealthier traditional houses, as in this picture. Known as a *thammat tang*, it is a development of the *thaen* in having a back rest and two arm rests. A distinctive feature is its depth; if used in a Western style of seating it needs a cushion behind to support the back. Because the seat was actually a platform and the monk sat cross-legged on it with his feet off the ground, it needed the extra depth. With its 'lion's legs', it may be used directly on the floor, as in the main picture opposite, or raised on a larger accompanying platform.

The most elaborate style of pulpit, and historically the most recent, is the *thammat yot*, also known as the *busabok thammat*. A *busabok* is a tiered reliquary, with a tapering top, for enshrining a Buddha image. This third kind of pulpit takes its name from its similar appearance. The elegant, tall structure, shown on right, is a tiered, wooden tower consisting of a base, body and apex. It looks far more like a Western pulpit than do the simpler seats, apart from the fact that it has a highly decorative appearance, the carved surfaces typically being gilded. The seat is within the body, and accessed by steps at the back or side, either built in or as a separate ladder. Spectacular constructions, they are too large and dominating to be seen outside monasteries.

Altar screens

สัตภัณฑ์
sattaphan

Left, top: Gilded triangular screen known as a *panjaroop*, or stand for hanging a gong, now housed in the National Museum at Chiang Mai. *Left, below:* A more primitive screen from the monastery of Wat Phra That Lampang Luang, near the town of Lampang. *Right:* Semi-circular screen, also in the Chiang Mai National Museum, with 28 *naga* serpents, their bodies inset with individual coloured glass scales, and the head of a guardian yak figure.

Candles are regularly lit and placed as offerings in front of the principal Buddha image in a monastery, and in the North a particular type of holder developed for this purpose. Known as a *sattaphan*, it comes in the form of a large, heavy screen, usually elaborately decorated, free-standing and intended to be situated in front of the altar.

As these screens were made expressly as merit-making offerings to monasteries, they were typically constructed with great care and skill. The best have intricate carving that completely covers the surface area, and there is considerable variety of style and execution. One consistent feature is that the screens have seven individual spiked posts, called *rao tien*, in which candles are placed. The significance of this number goes back to Buddhist cosmology and refers to the seven mountains surrounding Mount Meru.

The gilded triangular screen (left, top), known as a *panjaroop*, or stand for hanging a gong, measures slightly less than 2 m (6.6 ft) in height and slightly more than 2 m in width. It is from Chiang Mai, and is now located in the National Museum there. The outer edges follow the style of the bargeboard of a monastery roof (see pages 90–91) and are worked as a cascading set of three *naga*

serpents with rearing heads (one is broken off). The interior is filled with very fine *kanok* looping vines, carved as openwork and set against a painted board.

An inscription (which northern Thais in particular were fond of adding to offertory objects that were presented to monasteries) records that it was made in 1924 as a dedication to her husband by one Mae Kham Paeng.

The semi-circular screen on right, also 2 m (6.6 ft) wide and also in the Chiang Mai National Museum, is an exceptional piece of work, featuring a complex arrangement of 28 *naga* serpents, densely entwined, their bodies inset with individual coloured glass scales. At the head of the arrangement is the head of a guardian yak figure. The more primitive screen (left, below), painted green and red, is a much less sophisticated affair, but it has a certain naive charm. It is located in the monastery of Wat Phra That Lampang Luang, near the town of Lampang.

Scripture cabinets

ตู้พระธรรม

tu phra thamma

Palm-leaf manuscripts carrying Buddhist scriptures were monasteries' main treasures. Palm leaves, each measuring some 35–45 cm (14–18 in) by 5–7.5 cm (2–3 in), were first trimmed into long sheets, and then inscribed: letters were scratched into the leaves with a needle and ink rubbed into these letters. The sacred nature of the contents, the painstaking production and their uniqueness all made their preservation a matter of importance. Termites, and the heat and humidity of Thailand's tropical climate, were their enemies.

Thus, the manuscripts were stored in cabinets and chests in small libraries within the monastery grounds. The libraries were built to give maximum protection: they were raised high above the ground, often on stilts, or sometimes in a specially dug pond. The containers were, wherever possible, treated to careful workmanship and devotional art.

The principal example on right, from the Ayutthaya period, is now in the National Museum, Bangkok. It is generally considered as the finest example of its style—both in its proportions and the standard of its gilded lacquer decoration. This scripture cabinet is a product of the Wat Soengwai school, from the monastery of that name in Nonthaburi, a riverside town a little north of Bangkok. It is,

typically, almost square in plan; its sides and corner posts slant inwards towards the top, like the truncated base of an elongated pyramid. Most such cabinets measure about 120 cm (47 in) high (excluding the feet) and 90 cm (35 in) along the sides at the base; a peculiar characteristic is the base tapers upwards.

Among the qualities that makes the design of this cabinet so fine are the dynamism of its composition, the space-filling complexity, and the combination of decorative elements, principally in the form of the flame-like *kanok plaew* motif, with beautifully observed figurative detail. The scene is part forest, inhabited by animals, birds and mythological creatures, and part abstract ornament. Note the pairs of mythological lions, *singh*, embedded in the *kanok* foliage at the base of the door panels, full of demonic playfulness; squirrels and birds inhabit the upper levels. The four other cabinets featured opposite are in the national museums in Chiang Mai (two on left) and in Nan (two on right).

The advent of printing technology and the possibility of reproducing the scriptures saw much Buddhist art declining, and work on manuscripts, cabinets, even libraries, just stopped. Today, the cabinets take on a new life in domestic interiors.

Opposite: Four chests used for storing palm-leaf manuscripts, all intricately carved and decorated as befits their function. *Above:* Scripture cabinet from the Ayutthaya period, a product of the Wat Soengwai school, now in the National Museum, Bangkok.

Monastery drums

กลองเอว

klawng aew

The oldest instruments in all cultures are the percussion, and in most of Asia that means the drum and gong. Indeed, the Thais, like the Chinese, often refer to the two together in one expression: 'gongs-and-drums'. Naturally, instruments as ancient as these have acquired a range of uses well beyond their roles in an orchestra. In the case of Thai drums, of which there are about two dozen varieties, many are named after the activity with which they are associated. There are *klawng khon*, used to accompany performances of the masked *khon* drama described on pages 46–47, and *klawng nang*, used with shadow plays. Drums were used in the past to signal the evening hours, and in most northern monasteries there are drums for regulating activities and for celebrating certain ceremonies.

These monastery drums are the largest in Thailand, and have a highly distinctive, elongated shape, with a single drumhead and a narrow waist flaring slightly towards the 'tail'. The very largest can be found in Mae Chaem in North Thailand, shown in the main picture on right; it averages 3 m (9 ft) in length. Its Thai name, *klawng aew*, means 'waisted drum', and refers to the narrow central section where the two halves join. The resonance chamber takes up half of the length, tapering

slightly from the drumhead, which normally has a diameter of about 50 cm (20 in). The skin is held tight by groups of long leather thongs passed through twisted cane loops and secured in the middle of the drum, just above the 'waist'. The lower half of the drum is a separate hollowed-out cylinder of wood, carved decoratively to leave a series of protruding rings.

The drumhead, made of stretched hide, is usually painted with a black circle in the centre and a black rim around the edge, the paint coming from the sap of a tree. The black circle and rim help to mark the centre for the player, while the sap helps preserve the skin. In addition to this treatment, a mixture of ashes and cooked rice is sometimes also applied to the drumhead to adjust the tone and pitch.

The drum may be used for summoning monks to various activities, and also, because of the carrying power of its sound, to call villagers to certain ceremonies, especially in the most notable of events, the annual ordination of young men at the beginning of the rainy season, and at Songkran, the Thai New Year. There are drumming contests held in the coolest of the winter months: December and January.

A smaller version of the drum, also used in monastery ceremonies, is the *klawng yao* ('long drum'), about 75 cm (30 in) long, with a cloth strap that allows it to be hung around the shoulders. Both of these drums appear to have been adopted from the Burmese, and they are an equally common sight in monasteries around the Shan States of Burma. The story goes that during a lull in the bitter fighting towards the end of the Burmese wars in the late 18th century, Thai soldiers heard the Burmese playing this long drum, which the Burmese called *ozi*, and made similar drums for themselves. Another possibility is that Burmese immigrants brought it into the country during the 19th century. Whatever its origin, the drum is now very much a fixture of monasteries in the North.

Old drums are nowadays occasionally sold as antiques and also made into occasional tables; the wooden one shown on far right has been put to sculptural use in a Bangkok garden.

Left: Largest monastery drum found in Thailand from Mae Chaem in the north, a *klawng aew*, meaning 'waisted drum'. *Below:* Wooden monastery drum taking on a new incarnation as a garden ornament.

Monastery bells

ระฆัง
rakhang

Above: The monastery bell marks the time for activities, prayer and meals. Here, young monks at Wat Haripunchai have assembled for their midday meal. *Right:* Buddha image and monastery bell in a cloister at Wat Phra That Cho Hae, in Lampang. *Far right:* Bell-tower or *ho rakhang* with bell at Wat Yaang in Petchburi, accessed by a steep flight of steps, or a ladder.

The long drum is not the only instrument found in monasteries. Bells also play an integral part in monastic life and are used throughout the country. Their ringing, heard across the rice fields surrounding a rural *wat*, is in its way as evocative as the peals of English church bells. Thai bells, always bronze, are generally much smaller (approximately 30 cm [12 in] wide to one m [3 ft] tall), but there is considerable variation in size and shape.

At monasteries that are frequently visited by pilgrims and worshippers there may be a number of bells, often donated, rung by the faithful as part of their merit-making. Apart from these, there is the bell used by the monks to regulate the day's activities such as the example on far right in Wat Yaang, Petchburi, and on right in a cloister at Wat Phra That Cho Hae, in Lampang. Struck with a wooden baton or pole, this bell summons members of both the religious and lay communities to devotions at specific times of the day. It also tolls the day's end when monks assemble for evening vespers, and is used to indicate the noon hour.

As we saw on pages 72–73, monks rely totally on the lay community for their food: they collect alms early in the morning. The significance of the midday bell is to remind the monks that they are prohibited from partaking of solid food after noon: only liquid may pass their lips. The one other meal is taken at about seven o'clock in the morning, after alms-collecting. The afternoon and evening are given over to religious studies and prayers, and further meals would interfere with the concentration needed for these. The young monks from Wat Haripunchai, shown on left, have assembled for their midday meal.

This restraint is part of a general principle of moderation laid down by the Buddha; the scriptures contain a number of references to this. He said once: "I am restrained in deeds, words and food", and in addressing the King of Kosala: "Discomforts are less for a person who is always mindful, and who is moderate in food. He digests his food early, and he lives long". On the other hand, one of the scriptures says that a monk must finish all the food in his bowl so that he may receive water to wash it.

In the more important monasteries, the bell is housed in a special building: a bell-tower known as *ho rakhang.* Although there is no standard design for this structure, most are raised, with the bell hanging in a small space, sufficient for one person to strike it (as in the picture far right at Wat Yaang in Petchburi). It is accessed by a steep flight of steps, or a ladder.

Ceramic temple fittings
เครื่องประดับหลังคาวัด
kreung pradap lungkha wat

During the Sukhothai period, which probably began in the late 14th century, a series of powerful ceramic figures was produced as architectural fittings for religious buildings. These included the strictly functional, and those which, although practical, were regarded as embellishments. Examples of the first were water pipes for the irrigation system of the city; pillars and balustrades for walls; and tiles for roofs. The latter included wind-break finials for the ends of gabled roofs, and covers for the projecting ends of purlins. In keeping with their exterior use, the figures were not delicate in manufacture or design, but characterized by a rough strength and energy.

The ruins of only one Sukhothai site retain a few of their ceramic fittings: Wat Mangkon, the Dragon Monastery, which still has parts of a ceramic balustrade, as shown at opposite bottom right. The 'dragon' may well refer to, or have inspired, ceramic guardian figures that are no longer in place. However, despite the very few in situ traces, there are surprisingly large numbers in collections.

Notably, the decorative pieces, like those shown opposite above, have little to do with Buddhism, despite their being incorporated on monastery buildings. Common figures are dragons, fierce guardians and praying celestial

beings: *thewada*. The dragons are particularly striking as they bear no resemblance to any of the normal Thai bestiary used in religious art; they are certainly unlike the *naga* water serpents that feature so prominently on monastery roofs (see pages 92–93). Sometimes fired in two interlocking parts, the dragons may have been a kind of guardian; several were found at four ancient monastery sites, each located at one of the corners of the city of Sukhothai—perhaps an old belief brought down from the north with the migrating Tai settlers. Dragons suggest a Chinese influence, while the monstrous standing guardian figures probably have a Khmer lineage: at Angkor, pairs of statues guard the entrances to temples. The *naga* finial in the Ramkamhaeng Musuem, Sukhothai, on left, is of Sangkhalok ceramic. The pieces above are from left: *yaksa* or demonic ogre; angel gable finial now in the Ramkamhaeng Museum from Wat Pa Ma Muang, Sukhothai; four-faced finial from Wat Phra Pai Luang, Sukhothai; angel gable finial; and *yaksa* head, National Museum, Bangkok.

Indeed, the very use of ceramics as such architectural elements is ultimately Chinese, and contrasts with the Sinhalese and Indian influences evident in most of Thai architecture. One suggestion is the link was provided by Vietnamese artisans who worked at Sukhothai, rather than by any direct contact with China (for which there are legends but no evidence). Vietnam followed China in ceramic roof decorations as in much else, architecturally.

Whatever the origins, these substantial ceramic pieces are highly distinctive, most of them the output of kilns at Ban Pa Yang, near Si Satchanalai north of Sukhothai. The dynamic forms were painted in quite energetic lines, with brown and black overglazed pigment. Later, some kilns at Sukhothai itself began production, and these are unpainted, in pale grey and creamy white.

Opposite: Sangkhalok ceramic *naga* finial in the Ramkamhaeng Musuem, Sukhothai. *Above, from left:* A *yaksa* or demonic ogre; an angel gable finial from Wat Pa Ma Muang, Sukhothai, now in the Ramkamhaeng Museum; four-faced finial from Wat Phra Pai Luang, Sukhothai; another angel gable finial; and a *yaksa* head, National Museum, Bangkok *Below:* Wat Mangkon at Sukhothai, retaining a few ceramic fittings.

Monastery roof finials

ช่อฟ้า
chofa

If there is one single feature that epitomizes Thai architecture, it is the soaring, sweeping multi-tiered roof of monastery buildings. Thai architectural energy and imagination were invested into the country's religious structures, and these, ultimately, were the inspiration for most of the notable features of traditional house design. The culmination of the roof, both literally and aesthetically, is the curious, even enigmatic, ridge finial: the *chofa*.

Thai monastery buildings are noticeably embellished, but features like this finial are not simply applied decoration, but an integral part of the design. There is an established decorative order with a rich iconography; each element has a spiritual function. Some of these protect the building, others delimit the sacred space, others honour particular divinities, since in practice Thai Buddhism is quite syncretic. Creatures and beings from Hindu mythology, and even animism, put in an appearance. The difficulty with this very prominent finial— its enigma—is there is no agreement on what it represents, or even on what its name refers to.

The term *chofa* is made up of two words: *fa* meaning sky, which is appropriate for its position, and *cho* meaning either 'bunch' or 'tassel', which is not. It is not as if the shape of the roof has evolved from some kind of tassel

hanging over it, because all the historical evidence shows that the form has not changed in centuries. The record includes old bas-reliefs depicting buildings, some of them from 13th-century Angkor, which show the influence of Khmer design on Thai very clearly.

What the *chofa* represents is yet another matter. Most examples are derived from a mythical bird, abstracted to a greater or lesser degree. Some *chofa*, as here, are highly figurative; among these, many are clearly depicting a Garuda (*krut* in Thai), the half-man half-bird figure from the Hindu pantheon that is the steed of the god Vishnu and the mortal enemy of the mythological serpents known as *naga* (see pages 92–93). The Garuda sometimes appears elsewhere on monastery buildings, such as on the east-facing pediment, carrying on his shoulders Vishnu (Narai in Thai), and clutching the tails of serpents in each hand. To represent the Garuda again on the peak of the gable is quite logical, because the bargeboard, which decorates the edge of the gable and protects the ends of the beams, is often in the form of a snake, its head rearing up at the lower corners.

Other figurative examples are obviously not the hook-beaked Garuda; in fact, some are even called 'parrot's beak *chofa*'. The one

shown opposite is a mythological swan, the *hongse*, which also has a long history in Thai iconography, going back to the Mon Dvaravati culture. Stranger still is the *chofa* (third, above) gracing a monastery in the Nan valley in the North, which is a bizarre combination of an elephant and a peacock known as a *hasadiling*.

In the absence of any substantial written records of architectural symbolism, it is unlikely that the mystery of the *chofa*'s origin and symbolism will ever be resolved. What is known, however, is that there is a wonderful variety of interpretations, most of them involving stylization. In itself, this reduction to a purity of form is rather unusual in Thailand, where most design tends towards elaboration; thus it makes the *chofa* special.

Opposite: Chofa in the form of a mythological swan, or *hongse*. *Above, from left:* Three *chofa*—from Wat Chai Sriphum, Wat Chieng Man and *viharn* Pua (the latter being a combination of a peacock and an elephant known as a *hasadiling*). *Left: Chofa* with inset glass from Wat Chieng Man. *Above: Chofa* have even found themselves in domestic interiors as decoration.

Nagas

นาค

nak

There is perhaps no mythological creature that puts in so frequent an appearance as the *naga*, a water serpent with origins lost far back in time, before even the formal religions of Hinduism and Buddhism. Like the *chofa*, it graces monastery roofs, though in larger numbers. As we have just seen, its long, scaly body forms the bargeboard of several sections of the roof and is, wherever possible, gilded.

Naga means 'serpent' in Sanskrit, and its first documented appearance is in the Hindu cosmological myths. It also appears in Buddhist legend, reminding us how closely these two great religions were linked. Always, the *naga* had aquatic associations, and there was even a race of part-serpent, part-human *nagas* who inhabited the watery underworld. The most important legendary *nagas* had names. Ananta, also known as Sesha, supported the god Vishnu on a bed of its coils as the two floated on the cosmic ocean and the god dreamed the universe into existence. In another myth, the *naga* Vasuki lent its body to be wrapped around Mount Mandara so that the gods and demons, grasping its head and tail, pulled it back and forth, rotating the mountain and so churning up the ocean from which it rose to release magically the elixir of life. At Muchalinda, the *naga* protected the meditating

Buddha from a storm by rearing its large cobra-like hood overhead like an umbrella.

Its name shortened to *nak* in Thai, this serpent arrived with the Khmers who, at the height of their empire in the 12th century, controlled the larger part of what is now Thailand. Great stone balustrades, such as those at the Khmer temple of Phnom Rung, were the model. They symbolized a bridge between the world of men and that of the gods; that is, they marked the transition into the sacred realm of the temple. Much later, especially in the north of Thailand, the *naga* balustrades were copied as the entrances to Buddhist monasteries, as above at Wat Phra Kaeo.

Nagas, such as those illustrated on left at a gable end of Wat Pan Tao in Chiang Mai, or on right, on the roof finial of Wat Sri Khom Kham in Phayao, have a variable number of heads. There may be just one, three, five, even seven, but always an odd number. By and large, the Khmers preferred their *nagas* with multiple heads, and they used them not just as balustrades but also as acroters on the corners of their redented towers, and as the lower projections of arches, where they were almost always disgorged from the mouths of yet another water creature, the elephant-snouted *makara*.

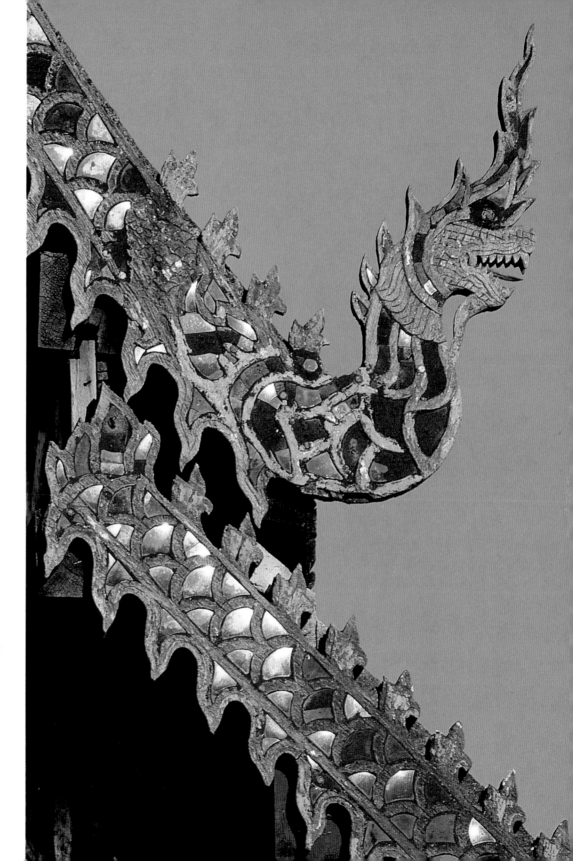

Far left: Gable end in the form of a *naga* at Wat Pan Tao in Chiang Mai. *Left:* At Wat Phra Kaeo, Chiang Mai, a balustrade in the form of a giant *naga* leading into the monastery. *Right:* Elaborate *naga* roof finial at Wat Sri Khom Kham in Phayao.

All of these architectural roles—entrance balustrade, roof finial and arch—were preserved by the Thais in their monastic buildings. Only the religion seemed to have changed, though what had actually happened appeared to be that one belief had been brought it to help another. In *Naga: Cultural Origins in Siam and the West Pacific* (1988), architect and writer Sumet Jumsai argues that the *naga* is made so much of because it symbolizes the pervasive aquatic rites and culture of the Thai people. Though not everyone would agree with his contention that Thailand is a "water-based civilization", Jumsai convincingly demonstrates how deeply such water symbols as the *naga* have permeated ritual and design.

He relates a rural measurement of the amount of water needed for the cultivation in any given year that is known as '*naga* giving water' (*nak hai nam*). *Nagas* use up water, and the more of them that are around, the drier the year. When water is abundant, only one *naga* is present, but in a severe drought there can be as many as seven. The monsoon, irrigation, flooding, and the watery network formed by the lower Chao Phraya River and Bangkok's canals (most now sadly filled in for motor traffic) all demonstrate an aquatic legacy, of which the *naga* is an appropriate symbol.

Eave brackets

คันทวย
kan tuay

The curved and flaring roof-line, so typical of traditional Thai buildings, serves two practical functions that are quite necessary in this tropical country: its height helps dissipate heat through convection; its shape copes well with heavy monsoon rains. The pitch begins very steeply close to the ridge, then becomes more shallow lower down to sluice the water out and away from the building—you have to experience a full tropical downpour to appreciate how well this design works. Not only does the roof itself curve gently, but there are usually also two or three distinct sections, each at a different pitch.

The lower roof projects some distance from the walls: this not only deposits the rain away from the foundations, but it also shelters any-one walking around the building. There are two possible structural solutions for these overhanging roofs. One is to build a surround of pillars, effectively creating a gallery on all four sides. This was a feature of large buildings in the Ayutthaya period, and later in the reign of King Rama III, such as in the Grand Palace in Bangkok.

This is, however, a costly and space-filling answer, and necessary only in substantial structures. For a more modestly sized building, a neater solution is a bracket attached to the

wall; this is what you can see on almost all monastery buildings. Traditional Thai houses from the Central Plains tend to use a plain bracket, often a pole sloping outwards from the balcony to the eave, but in religious architecture, the eave bracket has been trans-formed into a symbolic form in its own right, and a focus of artistic expression.

This focus is responsible for interest in the eave bracket, for otherwise, according to a Thai architectural historian, Professor Anuvit Charernsupkul, it "would hardly seem to be an architectural component that warranted serious study". Looking at the typical monastery building as a sculptural form, which its intri-cate decorative order encourages, we can see the carved eave brackets helping the overall form. They give clues to the scale, and in their repetition they link the diagonals of the roof to the vertical plane of the wall. The role they play lies somewhere between an independent piece of wood-carving art and an architect's structural device, and in some cases they have evolved to be primarily decorative, with the horizontal beam above doing the real work.

The most common motifs are the *kanok* vegetal design and the large family of floral shapes, and the *naga* that we have just seen gracing roofs and entrances. However, it is the

great variety and idiosyncrasy that gives eave brackets their appeal, as seen here from this selection of the monkey god Hanuman (far left) and the sacred goose (right). The picture above left, at first sight appears to be an intricate floral design but in fact contains the profile of a bird in a kind of illusion. In Thai this is called *kanok hua nok*, which rhymes nicely and means 'vine shaped as a bird's head'.

As well as the variety of individual expression, there are some distinct regional differences. Around the town of Petchburi, south of Bangkok, there developed a particular school of carving, which in the design of eave brackets produced the Praying Mantis style. In the North there is a variation known as Elephant's Ear, a triangular board which fits flush into the corner angle of the underside of the roof beam.

In the Nan valley in the easternmost part of northern Thailand, much of the art and architecture is influenced by immigrants, known as Tai Lüe, from southern China. Their contribution to the eave bracket is a varied and fanciful bestiary, all polychromed—often featuring different animals and scenes on each bracket around a building, such as that on right from Wat Bun Yuen.

Opposite, far left: Eave bracket depicting Hanuman, the monkey god, from the National Museum in Lamphun. *Opposite, top:* A kind of illusion is seen in this eave bracket called a *kanok hua nok* ('vine shaped as a bird's head'). *Above:* A traditional Thai wooden house showing eave brackets in situ. *Right:* Wooden eave bracket in the shape of a sacred goose from a house on Koh Samui. *Below:* Mouse and *naga* carving on an eave bracket at Wat Bun Yuen, Nan.

Carved door panels

บานประตูไม้จำหลัก

baan pratu mai chamlak

Thai religious buildings are sited on an axis, and both the *viharn* and the *ubosot* almost always face east, thus the long axis of the building runs east-west. In these symmetrical halls, the Buddha images are at the western end of the axial line, facing east through the doorway that is centrally located in the east façade. All of this gives a particular importance to the entrance, which quite often has a projecting portico, and so to the door itself, which can be treated as an architectural component. In keeping with the principle of symmetry, the door has two panels, and over the centuries these panels have become the focus of artistic expression. After all, the doors mark the transition between the secular world and the sacred.

The first point to note is that in many cases the doorway itself tapers slightly towards the top in a batter. This derives from a general characteristic of Thai architecture of the Central Plains, including that of houses, in which all four sides of buildings are intentionally inclined for stability.

With the exception of a few magnificent mother-of-pearl inlay doors and gold-leaf stencilling found in some monasteries in the North, the usual decorative technique is high-relief carving in wood. Natural weathering

gives them a limited life span, even when the material is the dense, termite-resistant teak of the North, but a few examples from earlier periods remain. One of the oldest (on left) is a long single leaf from a door at Wat Viharn Thong, Ayutthaya. Despite its weathered condition, it is a very fine example of the best of Ayutthayan art, probably from the first half of the 16th century. A central vine stem runs up the centre, in high relief, and from this emerge, at regular intervals, small divinities. On either side, foliage loops and curves down.

Broadly, there are two styles of carved monastic door. One features a guardian on each leaf, usually taking up most of the space; the picture opposite, right is an example of this. Most of the guardian figures derive from Buddhist and Hindu mythology (here, as in a number of instances, the iconography of the two religions converges), and some of them may have been inherited stylistically from the Khmer, who occupied Sukhothai among other places until the middle of the 13th century. *Thewada*, or minor deities, armed with swords, were a popular representation. Another was the fierce *yaksa*, a demonic ogre whose terrible aspect suited it to protective door duty. The rather bizarre figures on the doors of Wat Phaya Phu's *viharn* in the northern town of

Nan (left) are the work of local craftsmen and are known as *yama tut*. They illustrate well the diversity of carving introduced not only by regional and cultural differences but by individual skills and ideas.

The second type of door panel carving uses the many varieties of vegetative design worked into patterns—looping vine tendrils known as *kan khot*, thicker-stemmed vine motifs called *khrue that*, and several types of flowerhead—that forms the basis of so much Thai decoration. The top panel from Wat Pa Phra Men on facing page, top, is of this type, with the development of individual *thewada* figures ascending at the centre. A variation on this type has a mountain landscape at its base, representing the Himavamsa Forest of Buddhist mythology, and often features a royal breed of lion, the *rajasingh*.

Opposite, left: 16th-century single panel door from Wat Viharn Thong, Ayutthaya. *Opposite, top:* Top panel of a door from Wat Pa Phra Men, with vegetative designs. *Left:* Yama tut figures on the doors of Wat Phaya Phu's *viharn* in Nan. *Above:* Two guardians on each panel of a monastery door at Wat Phra That Haripunchai.

97

Door and window pediments
ซุ้มประตู, ซุ้มหน้าต่าง
sum

In the North, which in the main developed separately from the rest of the country until the close of the 19th century, monastery doors were further elaborated by what was called a *sum*: a carved pediment fixed directly over the entrance, right against the façade. Because of the abundance of teak in the northern forests, wood in Chiang Mai and the surrounding valleys was very much the dominant medium of construction. The North also produced large numbers of wood carvers. One can see in these pediments, which serve no structural purpose at all, an unrestrained display of skill.

Both pediments featured on right are famous examples from Wat Phan Tao in Chiang Mai. Employing both high and low relief carving and embedded coloured glass, a speciality of the area, the iconography is as complex as it is interesting. Over the main door, the triangular pediment is arranged around a stylized, full-bodied peacock, standing proudly, perhaps even aggressively. On either side, *nagas* with rearing heads cascade down, supported at the bottom by kneeling monkeys, while sacred Brahminy geese face inwards from the sides. A tiered *prasat*, or tower, forms the apex.

A curious feature of the pediment is the figure of a crouching dog straddled by the peacock. The explanation for this probably lies in the unusual origin of the building, which was the throne hall, or *ho kham*, of the fifth ruler of Chiang Mai, Chao Mahotra Prathet. The dog, which appears in the window pediment was probably the zodiacal animal of the ruler's birth year (the Chinese twelve-year cycle, with each year represented by a different animal, was observed particularly in the North). The hall was dismantled in a later reign, rebuilt and consecrated as a *viharn*.

The even more elaborate *sum* (on left) graces the scripture library at Wat Phra Singh, just a short walk from Wat Phan Tao. It is the finest example of a second type of pediment: attached to the front of the portico rather than to the gable over the actual door. Designed as a multi-tiered *prasat* with diminishing levels, instead of *nagas* undulating down the sides, there are a pair of dragons with feet, suggesting Chinese influence.

The doors beneath such ornate pediments tended to be treated more simply than the intricately carved panels (seen in previous pages), and typically are decorated with gold leaf designs applied by stencil. It seems that the emphasis has been shifted upwards, away from the doors. The origins of these pediments lie far back in Indian temples, even though the designs have evolved considerably. One of the clearest signs of this is the frequent use of undulating *nagas* to form the outer frame, with serpents rearing their heads on either side at the lower corners. In many cases, a pair of jaws just behind the neck of the serpent indicates a second creature, a *makara*, which is actually spewing out the *naga*. This identical treatment can be seen in India, in stone, in such places as the temples at Khajuraho, the Raths at Mamallapuram, and others. There it was the decoration of a functional element—the structural arch—and it probably came to Thailand with the Khmer, who made great use of it at Angkor and elsewhere.

Above: Tung hanging in a *viharn* in Wat Thai Fa Thai, in Phayao. *Top:* A banner hanging outside the entrance to Wat Pantao in Chiang Mai. *Opposite: Tung* are generally made from cotton, and are hung in monasteries or suspended from bamboo poles at festivals. This selection are made by the Tai Lüe people in Chiang Rai.

Buddhist banners

ตุง

tung

Called *tung* in northern Thai, these long cloth banners are a special feature of Lanna ceremonies, from festivals to funerals. They are essentially woven as offerings, both to the Buddha and to ancestors, and the latter belief suggests that these ritualistic hangings may have had origins that pre-date Buddhism.

The *tung* shown here are the most usual kind, woven from cotton. They vary in width from 10 to 40 cm (4–16 in), depending on the width of the loom, and can be of any length between one and five m (3–15 ft). When presented to a monastery, they are hung from the roof or a pillar of the assembly hall, but at festivals they may be suspended from long bamboo poles. At the ceremony known as *ngan poy luang*, to celebrate the construction of a monastic building, the banners will line the approach road for up to a few hundred metres (approximately half a mile).

While found throughout the North, *tung* are woven and used religiously with a special fervour by the ethnic group, the Tai Lüe. The Thais as a whole belong to the much larger Tai ethnic family, which includes groups in South Yunnan, Northern Vietnam, Laos, and the Shan States of Burma. Most northern Thais are Tai Yuan, distinct from the Siamese of Central Thailand, but the much smaller group, the Tai

Lüe, originally from Sipsong Pan-Na in China, have managed to maintain a strong, separate cultural identity. Most of them settled in the Nan valley in the early 19th century. The Tai Lüe monasteries are distinctive architecturally, and always contain inside a profusion of these long banners (see examples on facing page).

Both the Tai Lüe and the Tai Yuan elaborate their belief in honouring ancestors by considering the banner to be a ladder to heaven; for this reason most *tung* are divided into steps arranged vertically. Old palm leaf manuscripts recounting legends such as the Tamnan Muang Chiang Saen and the Anisong Tan Tang describe both the merit-making reward of presenting a *tung* to the Buddha and the way in which the ladder will help someone who has died and gone to hell to climb back out and up to heaven.

Typically, woven *tung* are white, with coloured supplementary weft, black and red being common. The most widely used motif is the *prasat*, the monument, which appears at the tail, or in sequence up the steps of the 'ladder', or as one long structure fitting the main section of a shorter banner. Animals, particularly elephants, usually accompany this as friezes. The patterns are generally applied by either the *chok* or *khit* weaving

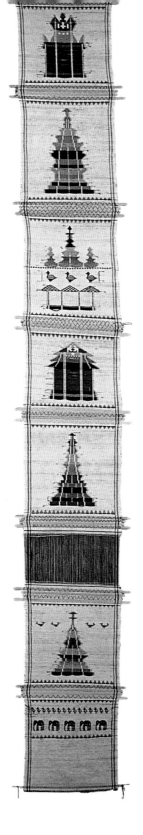

techniques. In the former, the supplementary weft is applied by hand to specific areas and is discontinuous.

Although most *tung* are cotton, there are a number of other varieties. One is a webbed *tung*, called *tung yai*, in which bamboo strips are included to give it a structure that recalls a spider's web: this is characteristic of Chiang Mai and its surroundings. In this, either large cotton yarns alternate with bamboo slats, or else cotton is bound around the slats. Paper, flowers, garlands and other items are added as decorations at intervals called *bai hai* (representing steps in the ladder) and at the tail.

Yet another, quite different style is of carved wood, usually teak. Such *tung kradang* are elaborately carved, and are either fixed to a post or placed on a pedestal. Some of the finest are displayed within the main assembly hall at Wat Phra That Lampang Luang, near the northern town of Lampang. The picture on far left shows *tung* hanging in a *viharn* in Wat Thai Fa Thai, in Phayao. The picture opposite top depicts a banner hanging outside the entrance to Wat Pantao in Chiang Mai.

Rural Crafts

Crafts of Daily Village Life

Functional vernacular craft is at the heart of the Thai tradition. The adornment it carries, as for example in the floral lintel designs for Northern houses, has a function rooted in spiritual and social necessity. Artefacts such as the Thai farmer's hat, the rice and seed basket, and shuttle for the loom are each a marvel of economy in design. Not only does form follow function—a Western 20th-century ideal that in Asia is more of a natural than a considered philosophy—but by virtue of the Thai aesthetic, such objects as these also display an elegance of line and shape that qualifies them as works of art.

Lanna gable decorations

กาแล
kalae

Top: The Kamthieng House, a northern Thai house that was transferred to Bangkok, sports a rather weathered *kalae. Above: Kalae* photographed in the Ancient City, Bangkok. *Right: Kalae* from Chiang Saen, Chiang Rai province, in the far north.

The northern provinces of Thailand, taking in the hill-country and intervening valleys, developed a distinct culture and art, and were not fully assimilated into the rest of the nation until the end of the 19th century. Geography, climate and the pattern of settlement set it apart, and its history is one of principalities established in valleys that were relatively cut off from each other and from the central plains. The collective name for the region was Lanna, meaning 'a million rice fields', and this word is still used today to refer to matters of style, culture and art.

The Lanna house, for example, was different in a number of ways from houses further south (unfortunately, we have to use the past tense here because there are almost no traditional houses being built today). The walls sloped outwards towards the roof, in contrast to the central plains houses where they sloped inwards. Equally distinct, to the point where it has become an icon of the North, is the carved V-shaped decoration at the peak of the gable, known as a *kalae.*

One of the best-preserved Lanna houses is, in fact, in the heart of Bangkok, in the grounds of the Siam Society. The rather weathered *kalae* in the picture on top left is from this, the Kamthieng House, originally on the banks of

the Ping River in Chiang Mai. The words *ka* and *lae* mean, literally, 'glancing crows'. This is clearly a little strange as, even if you exercise some imagination, it is hard to see any representation of inward-looking birds of any kind. There is a sufficient number of preserved *kalae*, mainly in museums and private collections, to be able to see stylistic trends, but none of them meet the actual description. In name and origin, the *kalae* is as enigmatic as its quite different religious counterpart, the *chofa* (see pages 90–91). To add to the confusion, the design is sometimes called *kae lae*, meaning 'glancing pigeons'. Whatever the meaning, the name has over the years come to be used to describe the entire style of house. *Kalae* dwellings were, of course, those of the reasonably wealthy.

There are three styles of *kalae*, distinguished by their shape. The first is a straight extension of the bargeboards, with very little alteration to the line of the projections. The second makes use of wider planks of wood which were then carved into a triple curve. The third style is an attachment rather than an extension, in the form of an 'X', rather stubbier than the other two in proportion, as shown on right. The design tends to follow the standard Thai decorative repertoire, in particular the *kanok*

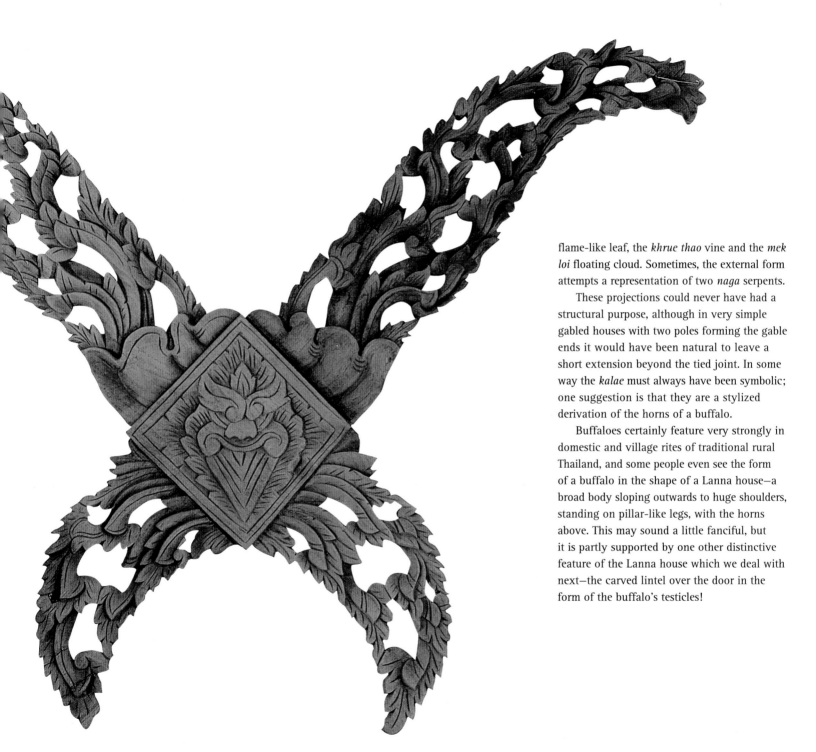

flame-like leaf, the *khrue thao* vine and the *mek loi* floating cloud. Sometimes, the external form attempts a representation of two *naga* serpents.

These projections could never have had a structural purpose, although in very simple gabled houses with two poles forming the gable ends it would have been natural to leave a short extension beyond the tied joint. In some way the *kalae* must always have been symbolic; one suggestion is that they are a stylized derivation of the horns of a buffalo.

Buffaloes certainly feature very strongly in domestic and village rites of traditional rural Thailand, and some people even see the form of a buffalo in the shape of a Lanna house—a broad body sloping outwards to huge shoulders, standing on pillar-like legs, with the horns above. This may sound a little fanciful, but it is partly supported by one other distinctive feature of the Lanna house which we deal with next—the carved lintel over the door in the form of the buffalo's testicles!

Carved Lanna lintels

หำยนต์
ham yon

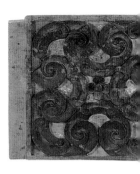

Much of domestic life in Thailand takes place at least partly outdoors, as befits the climate. Of the three divisions of the living area of a house, all of them raised on pillars above ground level, only one is an interior space. The terrace, open to the sky, is a working area and, in a large house, a walkway between different buildings. Raised about a foot above this is a covered veranda known as a *toen*, where most visitors are received, where meals are taken, and where the family generally relaxes. This veranda projects from the interior room, which traditionally is private.

In a Lanna house, the doorway leading from the veranda to the inner room carries above it a decorative lintel, carved in wood and charged with symbolism. Called the *ham yon*, it is designed to protect the family from harm—from both humans and evil spirits. More specifically, it protects the virility of the male householder and the fertility of the female. *Ham* is an old Lanna term for testicles, and *yon* comes from the Sanskrit *yantra*, meaning a magical diagram, thus 'magic testicles'. The testicles refer to those of the water buffalo, the animal closely tied to the fortunes and lives of farmers. This is one indirect piece of evidence supporting the theory that the *kalae* (see pages 104–105) represent the buffalo's horns. The examples here are fairly typical and have ornate floral and vegetal patterns that hardly depict testicles. The strongest allusion on the visible level must be the design of two symmetrical, roughly circular, whorl-like patterns, as in the picture on right.

There is a deeper symbolism, however. For example, as the *ham yon* protects the individual householder, its size is physically related to him. Its length must be three times or four times the length of his foot. Because it must also fit exactly over the doorway, the width of the *ham yon* is also determined by the owner's feet. There is an added depth to this, for in a Buddhist culture that deems the head the most respected part of the body and the feet the least, any visitor entering the room is, in a sense, debasing himself or herself by passing under the feet of the householder.

The carving and installation of the lintel is one of the rituals of housebuilding—or rather was, as the practice is now largely abandoned. In the case of a change in ownership, the old lintel is assumed to have accumulated power, but that means power for the previous owner. The new owner, therefore, must destroy this by violently beating the old lintel—clearly a symbolic form of emasculation—and then erecting a new lintel for himself and his family.

Opposite: House from the Chiang Mai Cultural Centre shows the *ham yon* or lintel in situ above the door. *Above and above left:* Two examples of lintels from Chiang Saen, Chiang Rai province, typical pieces with ornate floral and vegetal patterns.

Seed baskets and scoops

ปุง, ทัพพี

pung, tuppee

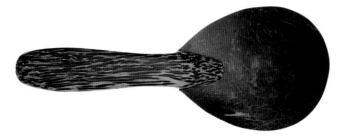

Rice is central to Thai life. The country is the major rice exporter in the world; at present, it sells around 4 million tons a year, some 30 percent of the world's trade. The Thais themselves consume around 128 kg (280 lbs) each per year, for, regardless of income, rice is their staple food. As it plays such a pivotal role in Thai culture, we have chosen two of the most basic artefacts to represent it: the seed basket and the rice scoop.

The sturdy basket on left, square at the base but round at the top, is from the north of Thailand. Called a *pung*, its very important function of storing and protecting seed rice is reflected in its construction. As the two enemies of rice are moisture and insects, the square wooden base is a defensive measure against both, raising the basket some 5 cm (2 in) off the ground or shelf.

As a round section gives more volume for storage than any other shape and is, in basketry, easier to make, the actual basket is round. However, in woodworking, it is easier to cut four straight sides than to turn a circular piece, so the base is square. In order for the basket to work upwards from square to round, a diagonal plaiting technique of bamboo strips was employed. Lacquer was also applied inside (black, and lightly) and out (decoratively, in several layers) to waterproof the container and to seal it against insects; the neck and lid are both deep for a secure fit.

Finally, the square wooden base is strapped tightly to the outside of the basket with rattan, which is secured to a ring just below the neck, and through holes drilled into the wood. The result is a secure container for the seed rice that will be used for the next season's crop.

The end of the rice cycle (which begins before planting and ends with consumption) is the rice meal, the foundation of Thai cuisine. In their own way, the Thais are as chauvinistic about their rice as are the Japanese about theirs, and the finest is called *khao hom mali*, 'jasmine-scented rice', which as an expression speaks volumes not just about the quality but also the way the Thais perceive it. Rice is as likely to be served with a cheap alloy spoon as with a more sophisticated implement (there is little ceremony in a typical meal), but we show above a spoon made of coconut wood. In its lines and construction, it displays the famous Thai flair for using local materials with grace and simplicity.

The rice it is used for serving is, by international standards, high quality long-grain, white rice, which usually commands a substantial price advantage. Indeed, the emphasis on grain quality is the main reason for Thailand's resistance to growing modern, high-yielding varieties. Its aromatic rice has traditional varieties with a history that goes back to the beginnings of rice cultivation. In fact, the earliest and most convincing archaeological evidence for rice domestication in Southeast Asia are pottery shards bearing the imprint of both grains and husks, discovered at Non Nok Tha in the Khorat area, dating from at least 4,000 BC.

Sticky-rice containers

ก่องข้าว

kong khao

Almost one third of the country's land area is in the highly rural, north-east region, as is nearly one half of the rice-growing land. However, soil erosion and drought during the dry season are acute, and the soil here has little capacity to hold water. The population is largely Lao-speaking, and among other characteristics, the people share with the Laotians a marked preference for sticky rice, otherwise known as glutinous rice—*khao niao*. Even in Bangkok, this is thought of as something of an oddity, and most westerners, if they know of it at all, think of it as a gooey Chinese dessert steamed in leaf packets.

It is the staple, however, for the north-easterners here—and many northerners too. The *khao niao* is eaten with the right hand, which pinches a small wad from the mass, kneads it between the thumb, forefinger and index finger into a kind of pad, and then uses this to scoop up a little food from the dishes served. A 'little' is a wise amount to take, as north-easterners have a predilection for extremely hot, spicy food.

For anyone unfamiliar with Lao cuisine, the description 'sticky' may give the wrong impression. Properly cooked, it is not gluey or gelatinous, but dry, with the individual grains adhering to each other. In fact, contrary to popular belief, the rice is not of a separate species at all, but rather a range of short-grain varieties with a waxy appearance and a very low amylose content. Amylose represents the amount of starch in the grain, and determines its eating and cooking quality. The dry, fluffy appearance of standard Thai aromatic rice is due to a high amylose content, whereas sticky rice has less than two percent in its endosperm and pollen starch. Both kinds are from the genus *Oryza sativa* L., the cultivated rice believed to have originated in Asia. Alan Davidson, former British Ambassador to Laos and a noted food writer, explains that there is no clear-cut distinction between the two; instead, "there is a more or less continuous spectrum of varieties of rice from the markedly non-glutinous to the markedly glutinous".

Family and close friends may simply take the rice from one central plate, but otherwise the rice is served in individual woven bamboo containers, in considerable variety, of which we show three here. The technique for cooking sticky rice is to steam it, never boil, and the secret of success is to soak it beforehand for a few hours. In markets and on the roadside throughout the north-east, you can see this specific way of cooking in a steaming basket known as a *huad*, as in the picture above.

From this basket, handfuls of rice are packed into the individual lidded containers.

The two baskets with wooden stands on right are both from the north-east. The older and darker of the two is double-layered in the traditional fashion for extra protection. In both, a carrying cord is attached to holes drilled in the base, and fed through loops on the lid, so that the container can be slung over the shoulder and carried into the fields by farmers. The simpler round basket shown below is from the north of Thailand, and is known as a *kong khao dok*. Its lid is attached by string, but it is not configured for carrying, only serving. The geometric pattern is achieved by dyeing some of the bamboo strips with ebony resin.

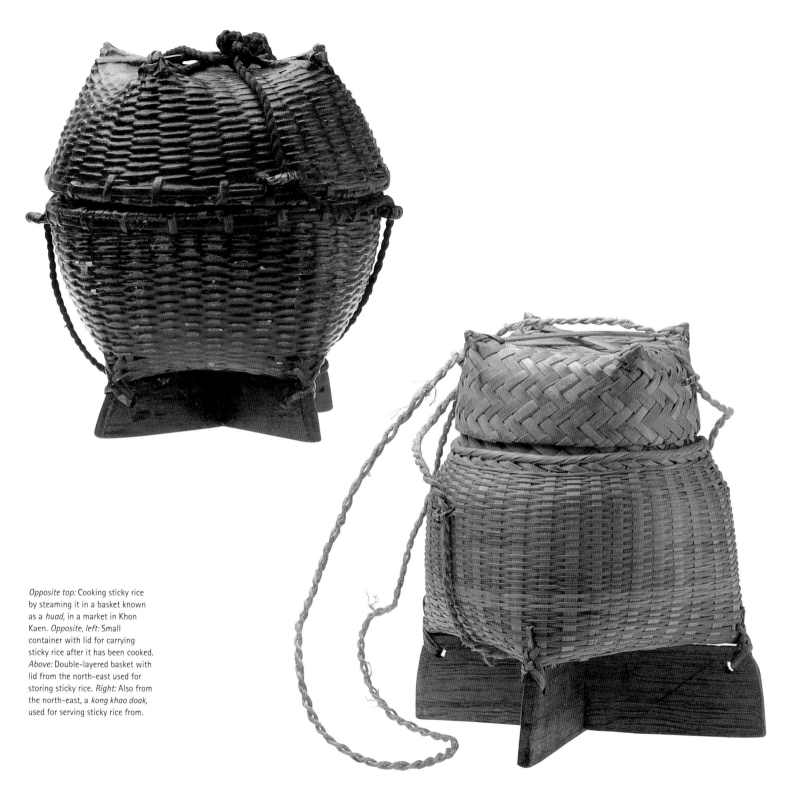

Opposite top: Cooking sticky rice by steaming it in a basket known as a *huad,* in a market in Khon Kaen. *Opposite, left:* Small container with lid for carrying sticky rice after it has been cooked. *Above:* Double-layered basket with lid from the north-east used for storing sticky rice. *Right:* Also from the north-east, a *kong khao doak,* used for serving sticky rice from.

Water dippers

กระบวย

kra buey

Thais are justifiably known for observing high standards of cleanliness—some might call it an obsession. Bathing and washing, whether of the person or of household items, are visibly frequent activities in Thai daily life, and all of this requires water. The provision and distribution of water in a traditional Thai household is a matter of some importance, and a number of customs and rituals attach to it.

Most of central Thailand is watered by the Chao Phraya River and its tributaries, rivers and *klongs*, which generally provide an ample supply. In fact, there is rather too much water in some years after a particularly active rainy season. In the past, most houses were close to, if not actually floating upon, water; as long as water was flowing, most of the family's needs could be served by simply reaching down from the terrace. In the north-east, however, where droughts are more common than floods, most of a rural household's supply would be collected and stored in huge earthenware jars placed under the eaves to receive rainwater. In the north, the usual source was a well within the house compound.

One of the easiest, and most informative, places to see the workings of a traditional Thai house, including the role of water, is in the heart of downtown Bangkok, in the grounds of

the Siam Society. Here, the Kamthieng House, a perfect example of a northern dwelling built for a wealthy family in the 19th century, was relocated from Chiang Mai in 1964. The well stands to one side of the raised buildings, and it was the duty of the younger women of the house to draw and carry water from it twice a day, using a bamboo basket caulked with resin to make it waterproof. The basket hung from one end of a counter-balanced bamboo pole that pivoted on the end of a post.

As seen on pages 132–133, Thais, strongly influenced by Buddhism, distinguish between upper and lower parts of the body in terms of moral ranking. High is superior to low, head is to feet, and the soul, or *kwan*, is believed to reside in the head. This affects the way water is distributed and used in the house, as it is needed for a variety of purposes, from drinking to bathing. Because the floor area of a house is used for sitting on, for eating from and other activities, it follows that one must always remove shoes before entering so as not to bring in dirt from outside. In a stilted dwelling like the Kamthieng House, therefore, footwear is left at the bottom of the stairs leading up to the terrace, and a bowl of water, with a dipper, is provided for washing the feet. This is the lowest 'rank' of water usage in the house, and for utilitarian purposes like this, the water is drawn from the well only in the morning.

The 'highest' use of water is for drinking, and this is drawn from the well in the evening. It is then placed in a 'high' position, on its own shelves on the terrace. Indeed, drinking water has its own small dedicated shed, with roof. There are two shelves, the upper for adults, the lower for children, and each has a few covered water jars made of porous earthenware (the porosity helps to cool the water by evaporation). Accompanying these jars are water dippers or ladles, as in the typical example here. Made from a small young coconut cut to slightly more than half, it is attached to a long carved, wooden handle.

Opposite, left: A water stand at Wat Si Khom Kham in Phayao, with a covered water jar and dipper close by. *Above and right:* Water ladle made from a small young coconut, attached to a long carved wooden handle. The form is functional, but attractive as well.

Coconut scrapers

กระต่ายขูดมะพร้าว
khood maprao

After rice, coconut is probably the most widely used ingredient in Thai cooking. Indeed, every part of the palm, including the leaf, trunk, nut and husk, finds a use in daily rural life. As we have seen, the wood from the trunk, combined with the hardened shell, provides a dense material for constructing implements such as spoons and scoops. In cooking, the prime contribution of the coconut is its milk, called *nam kati*, which is used to thicken and flavour different curries, meat, vegetable and fish dishes, and to create a range of sweets and desserts.

This milk is not the clear liquid found inside a young green coconut, which makes a refreshing drink. Instead, it is the liquid that is expressed from the white meat of a ripe coconut, and for extracting and shredding this, the Thais have developed a unique kitchen implement, the coconut scraper, known in Thai as *khood maprao*. It is basically a low wooden seat into which is firmly attached an iron grater so that it sticks out in front. To use it, the person grating the coconut cracks open the fruit and, squatting on the wooden scraper to stabilize it, deftly rotates one half of the coconut around the sharp end of the grater to extract the flesh inside. In one motion, the flesh is removed and shredded.

The next step in the operation is to steep the grated meat in boiling water, and then, after it has cooled, squeeze it to express the milky liquid. It is important to distinguish between two kinds of coconut milk: 'thick' and 'thin'. The first pressing of the moist shreds is 'thick', and this is set aside because it is used at different stages in cooking, and for different dishes. Repeated soakings of the shreds in water produce 'thin' milk.

No doubt the original scraper was a simple block of wood that allowed the user to sit in a more-or-less comfortable position while scraping. However, over the years, the Thais have elaborated the implement, usually to represent an animal. By far the most common animal is the rabbit—*kratai* in Thai—as in the picture on top right. Sometimes the scraper is called by its full name, *kratai khood maprao*, or 'grating rabbit'. The reasons for choosing this animal are quite obscure. One theory is that the sharp protruding iron grater recalls the prominent front teeth of a rabbit. Some support for this comes from the fact that in Laos a plain, non-animal type of scraper is used, and is still called a 'rabbit'. However, other animals are also depicted, such as the elephant in the main picture on right; even crouching people are sometimes represented.

Left: Coconut scraper in the shape of a rabbit or *kratai*, the most common animal for such objects. It is sometimes known as a *kratai khod maprao*, or 'grating rabbit'. *Below:* Scraper in the form of an elephant; the person sits on the back of the elephant to stabilize it, then rotates one half of the coconut around the sharp end of the grater to extract the flesh.

As often happens with genuine folk art, vernacular ideas and styles are guided partly by tradition and partly by individual quirk. And of course, this is a folk art that has all but disappeared in the face of more convenient and less menial methods of food preparation. The grating rabbit, elephant and the entire menagerie are now more likely to be found in an antique shop than in a kitchen.

Right, top: Celestial maidens at the annual Ploughing Ceremony in Bangkok carrying silver- and gold-painted gaskets suspended from elegant carrying poles. *Right, below:* Women carrying rice in the Mae Chaem valley in the northwest of Thailand. Their loads may exceed 20 kg, yet still be comfortable to carry in this manner. *Opposite top:* Typical pole or *haab* made from bamboo. *Opposite, below:* Typical pannier which is balanced on either end of the carrying pole.

Carrying poles

ไม้คานหาบ
mai kan haab

What more elegant and practical means of carrying rice around could there be than the pole that the Thais call a *mai kan haab*? As shown in the picture above, a shaped length of bamboo with a good diameter is all there is to it, but how perfectly it fits the purpose. Here, the elegance is not in embellishment or sophistication, but in the extreme economy of means. There are more decorative versions, as used in the annual Ploughing Ceremony in Sanam Luang (opposite, above) but the basic Thai farmer's model is completely functional. A no-nonsense implement, it allows women like these northerners from the Mae Chaem valley (opposite, below) to carry a combined weight of more than 20 kg (44 lb) quite cheerfully from the fields to the village.

One of the secrets of its construction is to find a sturdy, thick culm of bamboo, ideally not much less than 10 cm (4 in) in diameter, so that it will set comfortably on the shoulder and enable the load to be spread efficiently. The bamboo is first cut to approximately 140 to 150 cm (55–59 in) long, then split lengthwise, and finally carved so that it tapers towards each end. In a final clever touch, in order to secure the frames or cords for holding the panniers, a part of the nodes at each end are left as projections.

Sulpiz Kurz, writing in 1876 in the *Indian Forester*, described its use in Southeast Asia: "The bamboo halms are very strong, and can resist loads of 45 to 90 kg (100–200 lb), but if exposed too much to the sun are apt to crack on account of heating the air enclosed in their joints. Smaller [carrying poles] are made of a shape somewhat like bows, flattened and the edges rounded, often more or less ornamentally carved towards their ends. Loads of equal weight are fastened at both ends so as to keep the balance.... The carrying of such loads has its peculiarities, inasmuch as the carrier hastens in consonance with the elastic swingings of the bamboo, taking at the same time advantage of every swing that may lessen his burden. In this way he carries with less exertion a larger load than do the monotonously singing *palkee* bearers of Bengal, whose poles consist of unelastic wood."

The panniers balanced at the ends of the carrying pole vary in their design according to use. For rice and other bulk products they are simple affairs, but there is a more refined construction known as a *kra bung*, a basket woven of bamboo strips and reinforced by rattan, fitted with a base and four feet so that it will stand upright when lowered from the pole. This container, which may also be fitted with a flat circular tray for holding prepared foods for sale in a market or by the roadside, fits into an elegantly shaped carrying frame called a *sa raek*; the loop at the top of this frame fits over the ends of the pole.

The pole and its *kra bung* baskets put in a more elaborate appearance at the annual Ploughing Ceremony in Bangkok, a Brahmanic ritual to inaugurate the rice planting season (opposite, top). The King is represented by the Harvest Lord (a senior Agriculture Ministry official), who conducts the symbolic sowing of seed rice, from silver- and gold-painted baskets borne by four Celestial Maidens (also government officials).

Farmer's hats

งอบ
ngorb

Among the classics of basketry design must be the Thai farmer's hat, or *ngorb*. Looking like an upside-down basket, it offers good protection from sun and rain, and is also very comfortable, being lightweight and well ventilated. There may be other designs of farming headgear in the country, but the *ngorb* approaches the ideal more closely than any, and even in its completely functional form manages also to achieve a simple elegance, incorporating in its profile what must among Thais be an innate love of the curve.

The lack of variation in its construction across the Central Plains suggests that it is a long-established design. Traditionally, the hats are made within the farming community. In common with many rural crafts, their annual manufacture is a seasonal affair after the rice harvest. Made from the most accessible of local materials, bamboo and palm, the hat measures on average around 20 to 30 cm (8–12 in) in height. It consists of a bamboo frame made from flat bamboo splints. These are plaited so as to form an open mesh with six-sided spaces: structurally very sound in a way similar to the triangulated weave of the wicker ball described on pages 142–143. Thin strips of palm leaves are then fixed to the outside of the frame, over-lapping slightly and fixed with rattan.

The hidden success of its design, however, is that the hat proper sits on top of a light, expandable cylindrical frame—a kind of cap—which fits neatly on the wearer's head. This separation keeps the points of contact with the head to an absolute minimum, and allows air to circulate underneath the hat—a necessity when working in the fields or paddling a canoe under the hot Thai sun. The cap has an open weave with oblong spaces and is pliable enough to expand to suit almost any head size. Because of this, one *ngorb* can be used by all members of the family.

Quintessentially rural, the *ngorb's* benefits were not always immediately apparent; only experience of outdoor labour in the heat reveals its true value. Prince Narisaranuwatiwong, working on an archaeological dig in the 1930s, was mildly surprised at this revelation: "During one of my excavation excursions, I had the misfortune to suffer a blackout, probably on account of my wearing a woollen hat. I observe that the *ngorb*-wearing boat women going about their business in the sun and looking very cheerful…. *Ngorb* of course does not actually cover the wearer's head, for there is enough ventilating space between the cap part and the shade on top. Since I began wearing a *ngorb*, I have yet to experience another blackout."

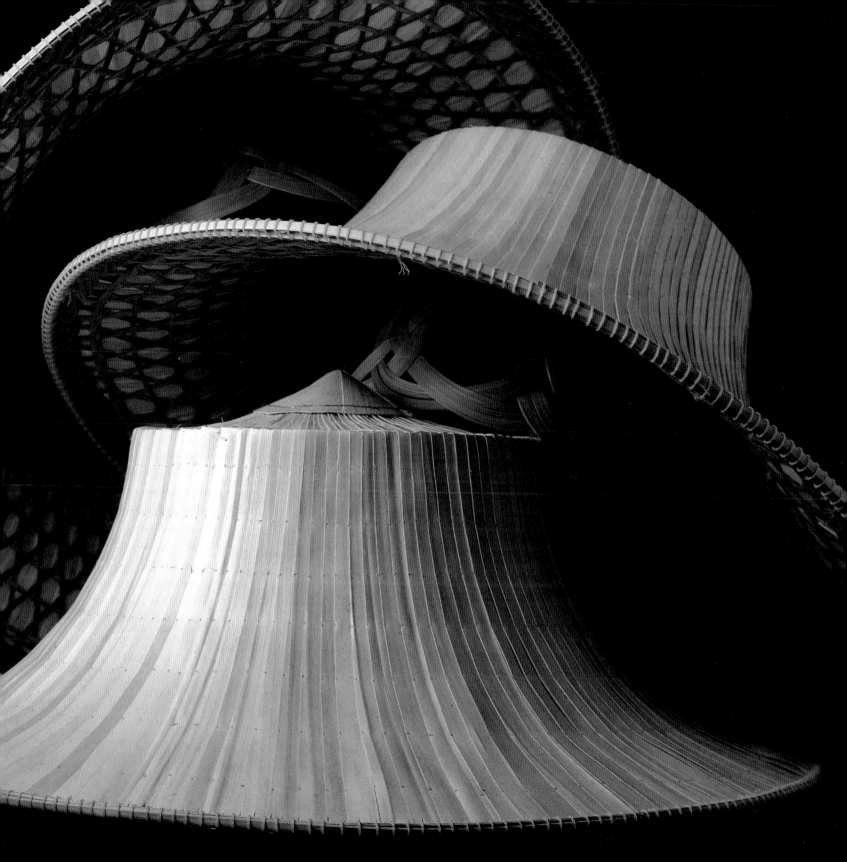

Poppy seed pod incisers
มีดกรีดฝิ่น
meed kreed fin

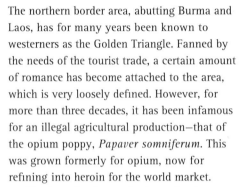

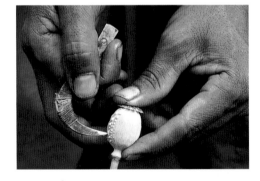

The northern border area, abutting Burma and Laos, has for many years been known to westerners as the Golden Triangle. Fanned by the needs of the tourist trade, a certain amount of romance has become attached to the area, which is very loosely defined. However, for more than three decades, it has been infamous for an illegal agricultural production—that of the opium poppy, *Papaver somniferum*. This was grown formerly for opium, now for refining into heroin for the world market.

The brass implement in the main picture on right, 14 cm (5.5 in) long, is an inciser, used to make the initial cuts in the poppy pod. It is one of a number of the tools of production, all of which are basic and functional, as befits an unsanctioned farming activity. The poppy thrives on poor soil and steep slopes at the higher altitudes of this region's hills, and was for many years the only realistic cash crop for the hill-tribes. The Lisu and Hmong in particular took to growing it, receiving a price for the processed (boiled) opium that could vary from around US$50 to US$120 per kg (2.2 lbs), depending on the size of the overall harvest, among other factors.

The poppy does not require much attention until the harvesting period, which occurs between November and February, just after the flowers bloom. When the petals have dropped away, a single pale green pod remains at the top of each stalk. This contains the milky opium sap, and the first step is to use the inciser to score the pod deeply. The inciser has two or three blades a few millimetres (0.2 in) apart, riveted together near the base and bound tightly near the top with twine. The twine can be unwound to allow the individual blades to be rotated slightly for sharpening. A day after the incision, the sap oozes out and oxidizes to a thick dark resin; this is then scraped off using a large flat blade with a curved edge, in an upward movement.

Opium consumption has been a habit in Asia since the end of the 13th century, when Arab traders introduced it to the Chinese; it was valued not only for its narcotic effects but also its medicinal properties. The poppy, being easy to grow, particularly on land that is unsuitable for most other crops, was an ideal cash crop for the minority peoples. However, its production did not become significant in this part of Southeast Asia until the late 1960s, due to two events. One was the 1967 ban imposed by the Turkish government, initiating a crackdown on what was then the major supply. From the end of World War II until the late 1960s, about 80 percent of the

international heroin trade was supplied by
Turkish poppy fields. Meanwhile, the hill-tribes
who had been migrating southward from China
and Burma after the war, brought this cash
crop with them.

The second event was the Vietnam War.
Opium refineries began producing high-grade
no. 4 heroin in late 1969, initially to meet
demand among American GIs in Vietnam.
After the troop withdrawals began in 1970–72,
production was re-directed to international
trade. The notorious Shan-Chinese warlord
Khun Sa even operated from a base in northern
Thailand until a Thai military operation
ejected him in 1982.

For the record, 'Golden Triangle' was the
American epithet for the opium-growing
region, which was approximately triangular,
with its base a line running from around Mae
Sot north-east to the border between Laos and
Vietnam and its apex in the centre of Burma's
Kachin State. It is now absurdly and quite
wrongly identified with the point where the
borders of Thailand, Laos and Burma meet, at
the confluence of the Mekong and Sai rivers.

Hilltribe textiles
ผ้าชาวเขา
pha chao khao

There is no shortage of exuberant attire among the hilltribes in the forested uplands of the North. There are six main groups resident in Thailand, and each has its own distinctive dress. Despite modernization, distinctive tribal clothing still continues to play a part in life among some of the women. Indeed, all the tribes have been able to use their textile and embroidering skills, to a greater or lesser degree, in the tourist market, even though this has led to some changes in techniques.

There are now more than half a million hilltribe peoples living in Thailand. The numbers are increasing, largely due to political repression in Burma, which shares Thailand's least developed border. Most of the migration took place in the 19th century, though the largest group, the Karen, have been living here since the 18th century, and the Akha from the beginning of the 20th century. Of the six tribes, the Lahu, Akha and Lisu are from the same linguistic group: the Lolo sub-division of the Tibeto-Burman language family. The Hmong and Mien speak Sino-Tibetan languages, while the Karen speak a Tibeto-Burman language unrelated to the others.

Dress is important in hilltribe culture as a defining element in cultural tradition; in all except the Karen, the most elaborate attire is

for young women of marriageable age. All tribes used to undertake all stages of the production process, from weaving to dyeing and decorating, but actual cloth production these days tends to be found only among the Karen and Akha. A few Lahu still produce their own cloth, but the other tribes rely mainly on cloth purchased from traders and stores; Lisu women's dress increasingly uses synthetic material, but in the way that they combine bright colours in their baggy tunics and tight leggings, they have maintained a highly distinctive style.

Homespun cotton is the basis of most traditionally-made hilltribe clothing. The care and attention that the weavers lavish on their textiles make their cloth highly prized for its strength and unaffected beauty—all the more so now that fewer and fewer women make their own material. The process begins in the cotton fields some distance from the village, beyond the surrounding barrier of unspoiled forest (these days eroded). Raw cotton is first processed through a simple gin to remove the seeds, then fluffed up by plucking a tightly strung bow. Small bundles of the cotton are then spun—a time-consuming process that the women usually fit into their other daily activities. Among the Akha, girls and women roll a drop spindle

against their thigh, then hold it up so that its weight pulls out the cotton into a strong thread, as in the picture on bottom right.

Once the threads have been combined to form a continuous warp—the lengthwise yarn—and in the appropriate season, when there is less fieldwork to do, the weaver sets to her loom. The Karen, who deservedly have the strongest weaving reputation, use a simple back-strap loom and a single-warp technique to create a variety of strong designs, some banded, others chequerboard, with red and white the most common colours. The upper garment is a tunic of very simple construction: two rectangular panels, front and back, stitched so as to leave slits at the top for the arms and neck. The old woman wearing such a tunic pictured on right is from the Pwo sub-group. Shoulder bags follow the same simple construction as the tunics, the two panels extending at the sides to form a broad strap, embroidered and tasselled.

Akha clothing also uses homespun cotton, but plain, and dyed repeatedly in indigo, taken from the surrounding forest, until almost black. The Akha use a foot-treadle loom, pressing on two pedals to raise the warp. The relatively narrow cloth is then dyed, which takes up to a month in order to achieve the

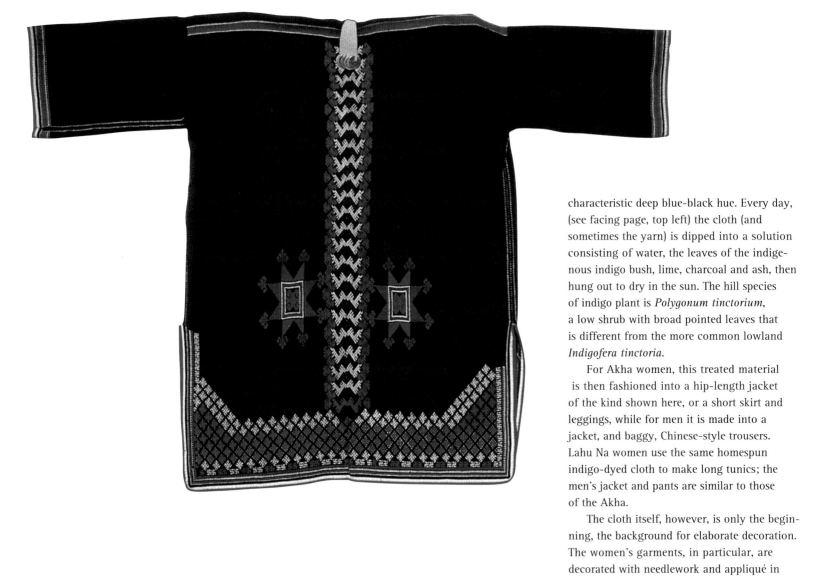

characteristic deep blue-black hue. Every day, (see facing page, top left) the cloth (and sometimes the yarn) is dipped into a solution consisting of water, the leaves of the indigenous indigo bush, lime, charcoal and ash, then hung out to dry in the sun. The hill species of indigo plant is *Polygonum tinctorium*, a low shrub with broad pointed leaves that is different from the more common lowland *Indigofera tinctoria*.

For Akha women, this treated material is then fashioned into a hip-length jacket of the kind shown here, or a short skirt and leggings, while for men it is made into a jacket, and baggy, Chinese-style trousers. Lahu Na women use the same homespun indigo-dyed cloth to make long tunics; the men's jacket and pants are similar to those of the Akha.

The cloth itself, however, is only the beginning, the background for elaborate decoration. The women's garments, in particular, are decorated with needlework and appliqué in strong, bright colours and geometric patterns. Patchwork appliqué work—which involves cutting shapes from different colours of cloth and then stitching them together—is a special feature of the Lahu, and the Lahu Na woman (see picture on top right of previous page) is

Opposite: Brightly dyed Akha jacket with geometric patterning. *Far left:* Cloth dyed with a solution from the indigenous indigo bush, lime, charcoal and ash, hanging out to dry in Maw La Akha village. *Left:* Jacket of a 'Blue Hmong' girl with bands of embroidery and appliqué strips stiched to the front. *Below:* Back of an Akha jacket.

working on a bag. The jacket of the Hmong Njua (more usually referred to as 'Blue Hmong') girl shown above, right, displays the typical 5- to 6-cm (2–2.4 in) bands of embroidered and appliquéed strips stitched to the front. She wears a black apron below this.

The Akha also use some appliqué, but their finest decoration is embroidery, in clearly demarcated horizontal bands. Some of these geometric patterns have a particular significance. The zig-zag line, a common motif in Akha embroidery and seen in the close-up picture on page 123, is called 'The Path'. This pattern depicts the switchback trails used by the Akha, who have little experience of flat land in their daily lives. Their villages are sited on mid-level ridges, and their existence, as with most of the tribes, is on slopes. In the Akha language, for example, there is no simple idiom for 'to go'. Instead, the expressions for walking and movement include the qualifiers 'up' or 'down'. Dr Paul Lewis, missionary and linguist, tells the story of his research when translating the New Testament into Akha; asking for the expression to walk along the level, he was told: "Oh, we never walk along the level. We are always going either up or down."

Decoration does not just involve needlework. The cloth shoulder bag has attachments of small silver buttons, known as *chukhaw*, and rows of cowrie shells (see page 122). Seeds of different types are also used, such as the white ones called Job's tears, which are the grains of a grass (*Coix lacryma*). Sometimes, even iridescent beetle carapaces put in an appearance.

Hilltribe jewellery
เครื่องเงินชาวเขา
kreung ngoen chao khao

Jewellery, and in particular, silver jewellery, plays more than a decorative role in hilltribe society. It demonstrates the wealth of a family, defines its status, and enhances the attractiveness of girls of marriageable age. In general, across all the tribal groups, wealth is worn rather than hoarded. Silver is the metal of choice: it is more affordable than gold for people who live in rather marginalized economic circumstances and easy enough to work into heavy, bright, jangling ornaments. Part of the reason for the hilltribe faith in silver lies in their history of uncertainty; over centuries, these people have had to migrate to escape persecution of one kind or another. Paper money thus often became worthless.

Silversmithing has been in serious decline for a few decades, and very few villages now have a resident smith. The job is usually combined with that of the blacksmith, who does of course have a regular flow of work, making machete-like field knives, hoes, sickles, spades and axes, and occasionally repairing long shotguns used for hunting. Modern silver work tends to be restricted to making buttons, studs and similar uncomplicated items, and the pieces shown here are essentially a lost craft. The raw material was purchased either in the form of silver sheet from Chinese or Shan traders, or as coinage. The silver content of these varies from about 60 percent for some Chinese coins to 92.5 percent for some rupees from British India.

Brass and copper are also sometimes used, and a recent trend has been to wear aluminium as a substitute. This has been a response not only to the higher price of silver, but also to what seems to be an increasing danger of robbery—the equivalent of a former Western practice of having paste jewellery made in imitation of the owner's real pieces considered too valuable to wear on most occasions. The decline in silversmithing was triggered in the 1970s, ironically by the sharp rise in the world price of silver. It became so expensive that robbers began to stalk hilltribe women and attack them outside their villages. The Akha women were particular targets because of the silver ornaments attached to their head-dresses. As we see on pages 130–131, the women traditionally never removed the head-dress, but wore it everywhere. At that time, robbery was a daily occurrence in some areas, encouraging the families either to sell their silver or hide it at home, fashioning substitutes from aluminium.

Silver nevertheless makes up the bulk of traditional jewellery, but it takes a variety of forms, according to sex and the tribal group. Surface decoration is not as sophisticated as the Thai work (see pages 28–29), but it has vigour and simplicity. Engraving and chasing (both worked from the front of the silver, the latter involving punching down the background to leave areas of design standing in relief) are the most common techniques, with geometric and floral designs predominating. Less frequent use was made of *repoussée*, appliqué, filigree, granulation and enamelling.

The two pendants overleaf, both on chains, are of the type worn mainly by the Lisu, Lahu and Akha women, around the neck or, more usually, from a shoulder loop or from the back of a neck ring. Both end in a set of personal grooming instruments hanging as pendants,

adding a practical feature to the silver's functions as investment and display. They include tweezers, needles, knives and brushes, a hilltribe version of the Swiss Army knife. The New Year's celebrations are still the occasion for bringing out the best jewellery–the fine old heirlooms–and for dressing up. In the picture (bottom of page 127), Lisu girls from a village near Tak don layer upon layer of necklaces, rings and studs.

Probably the most characteristic items of hilltribe silver are the neck rings and bracelets, shown above. For these prominent pieces, the silversmiths who made them insisted on the highest possible quality of silver, because they should never tarnish. They are worn by both men and women, and by most of the tribal groups. The Karen are the exception, eschewing heavy silver in favour of bead necklaces in great variety; their most common silver item is a necklace made of small-denomination old Thai 'bullet' coins (see pages 24-25).

Each tribe in the other five main groups has certain preferences in design. The plain flat neck ring (top, first from left) with recurved spiralling ends is worn by Akha women. The round solid ring with long recurved and engraved ends in the shape of a bird's beak (top, second from left), are widespread among the Hmong, Mien, Lahu and Akha, while the torque in third from left on top, similar to this round solid ring but twisted, is worn by the Hmong (the Lahu also wear torques, but the twisting is tighter). Finally, the much thicker rings (top, right), bulging towards the centre, are hollow and worn mainly by the Hmong and Mien, sometimes by the Akha.

The group of bracelets on page 126, some in pairs as they were normally worn, includes both solid and hollow examples. The twisted-wire designs in the centre are mainly of Chinese origin, and worn especially by Akha women of the Pa Mi sub-group; the hollow designs, some engraved (one with its date) are worn mainly by Lahu and Akha men, while the small solid ring with the twisted-wire clasp is of the type worn by Wa/Lawa people. The chunky bracelets worn by men have yet another purpose, to protect the wearer from harm, and the most highly regarded are the Chinese-influenced designs with dragon heads at each end, and between 1 to 2 cm (0.4–0.8 in) in diameter. They are intended to rattle with movement, and the hollow ones usually contain a loose ball or pellet that rolls around inside and adds to the noise.

The origin of many of the silver pieces in the possession of hilltribe peoples has been

obscured by their itinerant existence; they may have been purchased from the Chinese or Shan, or they may have been made by tribal smiths to similar designs and with acquired techniques. One old Akha man interviewed explained: "Our silversmiths have always learned from our neighbours. When we lived among the Chinese, they made silver that was like that of the Chinese; and when we were neighbours of the Shan, our silver resembled that of the Shan." The enamelling on the necklace on far left certainly suggests a Chinese origin, but long ago some particularly adept Lisu or Akha silversmith probably learned the process. What is certain is that today in Thailand none of the hilltribe communities have silversmiths capable of working to the same standards displayed in these old pieces.

Opposite, far left and right: Two pendants, both on chains of the type worn mainly by the Lisu, Lahu and Akha women; both end in a set of personal grooming implements. *Opposite, above:* Four neckrings or torques worn by the Akha, Hmong, Mien and Lahu. *Above:* Wedding jewellery of the Lisu; sadly the workmanship displayed by the old silversmiths who made these pieces is a declining skill.

Akha head-dresses

หมวกของหญิงเผ่าอะข่า

muak khong ying phao Akha

Top: Using buffalo horn to make the Akha silver head-dress. *Above:* Woven bracelet being dyed with the crushed leaves of a forest plant. *Opposite, top:* Head-dress from the Pa Mi Akha. *Opposite, right:* Magnificent Akha head-dress made by the wife of the local 'teacher/leader' in Maw La Akha village.

This ornate confection of silver, beads, chicken feathers, gibbon fur and bamboo, in the main picture on far right, is the head-dress of an Akha hill-tribe woman. If there were a world league table of tribal finery, the Akha head-dress would surely rank close to the top. More than a hat, it denotes status, wealth, and the tribal sub-group. It is a permanent item of adornment; by custom, a woman even sleeps in her head-dress, removing it only to wash her hair (in the old days, when all Akha women wore traditional dress, the sight of a girl's hair was considered erotic for a man).

The example on far right was made by the wife of the *pima* (the village 'teacher-leader') in the settlement of Maw La Akha, in the country's northernmost province, Chiang Rai. Not only does the style of the head-dress differ according to individual expression—depending on which ornaments catch a woman's fancy—but it also varies between the sub-groups. In Thailand there are three sub-groups, and this head-dress is from the U Lo Akha group (the most common). It comes in two parts: below is a wide headband of cloth decorated with alternating rows of beads and silver buttons, and hung with coins. Above is a bamboo cone that is even more profusely decorated: the Akha call it the 'pointed head-dress'.

The magnificent overall effect is achieved by layering a variety of textures and materials. Personal wealth is represented by the amount of silver on the head-dress. Traditionally Akha women have preferred wearing their assets to hoarding them, so in the 19th century, when the U Lo Akha were living in the Shan States of Burma, coins became the principal source of silver. This head-dress has Victorian and Edwardian rupees from the Indian Empire. Another group, the Loi Mi Akha, treat their silver in a different way, using a form hollowed out of a water buffalo's horn to hammer the coins into thin hemispheres (see left, top), which are then joined into hollow balls. An example of a head-dress from the third group—the Pa Mi Akha—is shown on facing page, top. Here the silver coins are French piastres and Indian rupees.

Invention takes the place of value for the most colourful ingredients. The tassels hanging from the top and sides are nothing more than chicken feathers, dyed red with the crushed leaves of a forest plant (see left, below) and then teased out. The circular bands on the cone are of woven bamboo, and the white seeds are those known as Job's tears. Gibbons—when these primates were still abundant in the hills—furnished the tufts of fur at the back.

There is an irony attached to this adornment and the situation in which the Akha find themselves. Thanks to the Thai tourist industry, this head-dress is internationally well-known, having been used extensively in publicity—indeed, it is chosen as an icon by the national tourist organization. Yet, ethnically speaking, the Akha are not Thai at all, and have had a difficult time settling in the country. Like most hilltribes, they are a marginalized people, moving through the uplands not through choice but to avoid persecution.

Their origins are obscure: for many centuries they lived mainly in Yunnan, and before that probably in eastern Tibet. Their language is from the Lolo branch of the Tibeto-Burman family, quite dissimilar from Thai. In a sense, they arrived in Thailand as refugees, and it has not been easy for them to legitimize their status. In recent years, however, an increasing number have been granted Thai citizenship, and for this the Akha can thank, in part at least, their new-found, if unsought, role as an asset to tourism, not least because of their exotic attire.

Triangular cushions

หมอนขวาน
maun kwan

Above and opposite: The ubiquitous triangular cushion or *maun kwan*, traditionally placed on the floor on a mat, acts as a side support to the arm, or as a back rest. It is stuffed with kapok and sometimes has an added folding mattress section for extra comfort.

As in Japan, traditional seating arrangements in a Thai house do not include actual seats. Life is lived on the floor, which of course has far-reaching effects on custom and etiquette as well as on proportion and viewpoint. It should be emphasized that this is traditional rather than modern, and there is obviously some decline nowadays in this lifestyle, more so in the cities than in the countryside. There is no successful way of combining floor seating and chairs, for certain specific cultural reasons.

In Buddhist societies, the head is deemed the highest part of the body, morally, and the feet the lowest, and Thais take great care to respect this situation. It is thus deeply insulting to pat someone on the head in Thailand; this is, of course, not something that most people would do in any society, and hardly worth mentioning except that it is also impolite to place yourself above another person. It is quite common at formal gatherings, for instance, to see Thais stooping as they pass others who are seated, as a gesture acknowledging this etiquette. "Noble head, ignoble feet", as one saying has it.

Add this religious view of the body to Thai social hierarchy, which is more stratified and pronounced than it now is in the West, and you can see that Thai living is more comfortable for all concerned when conducted on one level. The word for chair in Thai is in fact a Chinese term, and in the past such raised seating was reserved for two classes of society: royalty and the monkhood. The monk's chairs on pages 78–79 are appropriate because of the higher status, while a royal seat has its own special term in Thai royal language—*phra thi nang*: the place where the Lord sits.

These special cases apart, traditional daily life is, as mentioned, played out on the floor of the house, which is naturally kept swept spotlessly clean, and must not be sullied by dirt brought in from outside. For this reason, shoes are removed before a person enters a house. Mats are placed on the floor, and raised surfaces that are needed for such activities as eating, writing, or applying make-up are appropriately low (see pages 32–33). And needed for comfort is a low cushion that will not slide about; the Thai invention is function-ally perfect while aesthetically pleasing: the triangular cushion, or *maun kwan*.

Carl Bock, who travelled in the country in the 19th century, wrote of the arrangements in a well-to-do Thai house in 1888: "The best mats are edged with a red border and the cushions, which are either oblong or three-sided, have their ends embroidered in silk or

gold. When a visitor enters a mat is spread on the floor, with a cushion either behind to lean against, or at the side as a support to the arm—the quality of the cushions and mats selected depending entirely upon the rank of the visitor. The Chows (rulers) have, as a rule, a table and a few chairs but seldom use the latter except when visited by 'distinguished strangers' when they look very uncomfortable as they sit across legged on the seat."

The triangular cushion is densely packed with kapok, and inclines at just the right angle to support the side when sitting. For lightness, it is composed of individual triangular sections joined at the corners, and sometimes, as in the top picture on far left, with an added folding mattress section for extra comfort.

Shuttles

กระสวย
kra suey

With its elegantly tapering, gently upturned ends, the wooden shuttle or *kra suey* is, in its simplicity, a symbol of both the fundamental place of weaving in traditional Thai rural society and the insistence of Thai craftsmen on giving an aesthetically pleasing form to even the most basic of implements. Regrettably, most visitors to Thailand now see the shuttle being sold in Bangkok's weekend market as a kind of candle holder (with the candle filling the central bobbin cavity), and it is entirely probable that many have no idea about its original function.

The shuttle varies in length according to use, from around 25 cm (10 in) for fine tapestry weaving up to 50 cm (20 in) for plain weaving. Its ends taper, giving the overall canoe-like shape. The bobbin is placed in a cavity in the centre, and the yarn, which will form the weft, is wound around it, while the ends of the spindle fit into two grooves in the upper surface of the shuttle.

The role of the shuttle is to insert the cross-weave or the weft between the lengthwise yarn (the warp). The basic equipment for weaving in a Thai farming community, usually located in the general working and storage space beneath the stilted houses, is a standing loom, a simple rectangular box-like structure that averages 3.5 m long by 1.5 m wide by 1.5 m high (138 x 59 x 59 in). Essentially, the loom is a frame for tensioning the warp, which is secured at the far end, and around a beam just in front of the weaver's waist.

In weaving, the weft is interlaced between alternate threads of the warp—this is the job of the shuttle—and to separate the alternate threads of warp, each set is lifted by means of heddles, which are lengths of cotton (or, nowadays, often nylon) attached to the individual warp threads. The heddles are connected to a frame known as a heddle shaft, and this is raised and lowered by cords that pass through pulleys overhead. A plain weave uses two heddle shafts, which are raised in turn by means of foot treadles attached to the cord that passes through the pulleys. The shuttle, carrying the weft on its bobbin, is passed from right to left and back again through the gap in the warp, as in the picture on right. A beater, like a comb, is then used to press the newly inserted weft into the weave.

This is the simplest system of all, but for complex patterns, up to 16 heddles may be used. In the early 19th-century mural painting showing two women and a loom from Wat Phumin in Nan Province (on right), there are four heddle shafts operated by the weaver's feet; the shuttle lies next to her, waiting to be picked up once she has finished using the beater.

Weaving in Thailand is traditionally a female skill. Men make the weaving equipment, but the operation of the loom is strictly the women's preserve. Traditionally, a girl's proficiency at weaving increased her value as a bride, and some of the sayings from the north-east, the most rural part of the country, reflect this, even though to modern ears they also evoke a more conservative, proscribed way of life: "A good wife is like a ploughshare. If she is skilled at weaving, then her husband can wear fine clothes. A wife who talks harshly and is unskilled at her loom makes a family poor and shabby in dress."

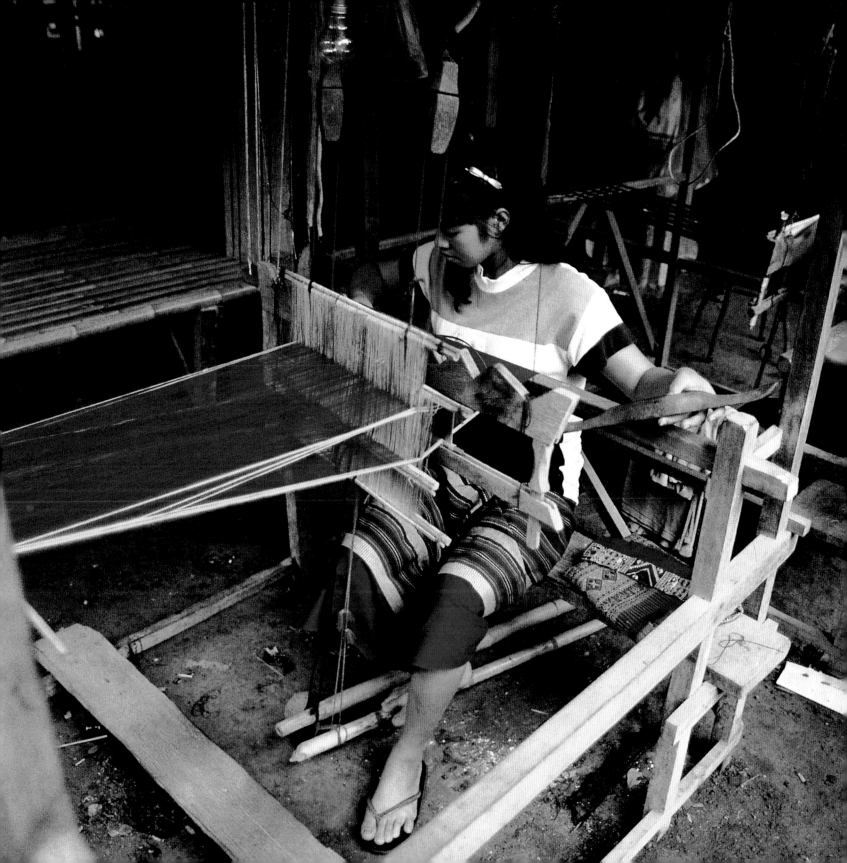

Tube skirts

ผ้าซิ่น

pha sin

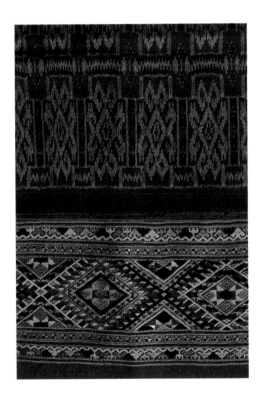

The principal item of traditional women's dress is the *pha sin*. This is a long, tube-like skirt that resembles the sarong, but differs from the latter in that the cloth is always sewn together at the vertical edges. At the waist the skirt is tied either by folding the fabric from left to right or vice-versa, or by making two folds that cross over at the front. In both cases the cloth is then tucked and rolled over, sometimes with a silver belt worn over the fold. In earlier times in the villages, as depicted in the mural painting from Wat Phumin in Nan, above, the *pha sin* would essentially comprise the entire dress; it was common for women to go about bare-breasted; they sometimes used a light shoulder cloth to cover one breast or—for visiting the monastery—to tie horizontally across both breasts.

As with traditional dress in many other cultures, the *pha sin* is fast disappearing from daily life, and apart from the most rural areas is more or less reserved for formal occasions—and hotel and restaurant staff, which actually is where most foreign visitors see it. In the case of Thailand, this inevitable historical process was hastened after World War II by the Phibun government, which encouraged Westernization in various forms, including dress for both men and women. In one sense, the *pha sin* was

marginalized by this, as it became associated with servants and low social status, and it is only since the 1960s that there has been a revival—but then only for special occasions. Nevertheless, high quality textiles everywhere have benefited from tourism, even if the uses they are eventually put to in the West are not quite those of their origin.

The *pha sin* has three parts: the waist band, the main body and the hem piece. The most common designs for the main body are either plain or with horizontal stripes; in the latter case they are part of the warp, evenly spaced and with one side seam. Because of the way in which the *pha sin* is worn—wrapped around and sewn into a tube—its length is determined by the width of the loom. The separate pieces for the waist and hem make up the difference.

The two examples here are more elaborate, both featuring intricate designs in the main body; both are from the fine private collection of Duang Jit in Chiang Mai. The *pha sin* on left is a late 19th-century Lao Krang (Lao-influenced) design, with the main body using the *mat mi* technique—*ikat*, or tie-dyeing—for which the Lao of the Khorat plateau and around Pakxé were well known. In tie-dyeing, the yarns are tied into knots with water-resis-

tant strings to resist the dye into which the entire cloth is dipped; they are prepared with the pattern before weaving. The picture shows the lower part of the main body and the hem attached below it.

The pattern in the main picture, also from the late 19th century, is from the Tai Lüe of Nan Province. The Tai here were famous weavers with a distinctive style that typically featured, as here, zig-zag bands known as *nam lai*, or 'flowing water'. Again, the hem is the lozenge pattern at the base. Overleaf, we take a closer look at hem designs, in which the greatest amount of work and artistry are concentrated.

Opposite, left: Late 19th-century Lao influenced *pha sin*; the main body of the cloth is made using the *mat mi*, or tie-dyeing technique. The hem is a separate attachment. *Opposite, above:* Mural from Wat Phumin in Nan showing women wearing *pha sin*. *Left:* Late 19th-century *pha sin* from the Tai Lüe of Nan province; the main body of the skirt features zig-zag bands known as *nam lai* ('flowing water').

Skirt hems

ตีนจก
tin chok

Opposite: Detail of a *tin chok* from Ban Thong Fai in the Mae Chaem valley. It features very densely woven narrow lozenges bordered by repetitive bands. *Left:* Modern hem from the private collection of Duang Jit. *Below:* Contemporary hem for a *pha sin* featuring raised embroidery in the Burmese style.

The difficulties of operating a wide loom undoubtedly had an influence on the structure of the tube skirt, as the standard width of cloth woven in rural communities would not cover the full length of a woman's leg, but tradition dictated that it should be ankle length. While the waist band, separately attached, concealed unsightly folds and bulges above, a hem was necessary at the base. One advantage of this was that the main body could be made elaborately, or with a fine yarn-like silk, while the waist band and hem could be made with tougher material that would wear better and could be replaced when frayed. Beyond this strictly functional requirement, however, Thai weavers made the hem a canvas for their decorative techniques, a way of displaying their expertise.

The term for this hem in Thai is *tin chok*: *tin* meaning 'foot' and *chok* a northern term meaning to 'pick', or 'pick out', which refers to the technique of pulling up individual yarns on the warp in which to insert special supplementary weft thread. This is done with a stick, or a porcupine quill, or just the fingers, and enables the weaver to introduce individual elements of pattern or picture. In effect, it is a kind of embroidery performed while the cloth is still on the loom, and in textile terminology is known as a discontinuous supplementary weft technique. With sufficient time and care and a good pair of eyes, it allows for extremely intricate detail and individual design.

The *chok* procedure contrasts with another principal technique called *khit*, which is a continuous supplementary weft. The former demands a preconceived pattern, which is created with a set either of shed sticks placed in the warp, or extra string heddles. With sticks, the pattern could be used only twice (first when the sticks were inserted in the warp, and then again when they were removed in reverse order). Heddles for the supplementary weft were a labour-saving device, but they restricted the complexity of designs, as the individual patterns were restricted to the number of heddles that the weaver had available, even though the order in which they were used allowed limitless combinations. But neither method compared with the extraordinary complexity that could be attained with the *chok* technique; some antique specimens show evidence of up to 1,000 shed sticks having been used.

Typically, the hem is in two design sections: a lower plain part, often red, with a supplementary woven part above, often on black. Lozenges are the most common design motif, and the woven section is finished with hanging 'tails' called *hang sapao*.

The main picture shows a detail of a *tin chok* from one of the very few villages with a continuous history of hem-weaving, Ban Thong Fai in the Mae Chaem valley, an hour or so's drive south of Chiang Mai. This is one of three main design structures used in the valley, and features very densely woven narrow lozenges bordered by repetitive bands. The *hang sapao* always alternate in black and white in the designs from this region. This painstaking work is a little easier when the hem is woven face-down, but still, a dense piece such as this can take an experienced weaver two to three months to complete. Two other modern hem designs are shown at top and bottom on this page.

Scarves

ผ้าสไบ

pha sabai

Top: Modern silk *pha sabai*, Chiang Mai style. *Above:* Mural from the Viharn Lai Kham, Wat Phra Singh, Chiang Mai, showing a woman wearing a scarf casually draped over the shoulders. *Top, right:* Ceremonial neck scarf of a Tai Lüe man. *Opposite:* 60-year-old ceremonial Lanna *sabai* from Nan Province.

Scarves completed the traditional dress of the North. As mural paintings show—the detail here is from Viharn Lai Kham at Wat Phra Singh in Chiang Mai, painted in the early 19th century—both men and women went more or less naked from the waist up. The two principal exceptions were in the cold season, when extra material was needed for comfort, and for ceremonies, special occasions and formal visits.

The solution was a scarf of one kind or another, worn in a number of ways. This is clearly a very old tradition, given that figurines from the Dvaravati period, sometime between the 6th and 11th centuries, found at Wat Khu Bua in Ratchaburi, show women wearing a sash over one shoulder, above light-fitting ankle-length skirts.

Probably the best known is the *pha sabai*, called *pha biang* in northeast Thailand, a long rectangular cloth for women. In the mural from Wat Phra Singh (on left) the woman wears it casually draped around her neck, both ends hanging down at the front over both breasts. Being bare-breasted was by no means indecorous until around the early 1920s, when Princess Dararasami, who had been King Rama V's consort, introduced blouses as official dress (known as *suea kho ya wa*, literally 'blouse with a Javanese neckline') in Chiang Mai.

Photographs from around 1900 show women wearing the scarf over one shoulder, covering just one breast (a position known as *saphai laeng* or *biang lai*), or horizontally around both breasts, in temples, in deference to the Buddha and monks. As temple festivals were ideal occasions for people to dress their best, the scarf developed into a highly fashionable item of attire. The silk scarf with gold embroidery above would be such a piece: in the collection of Khun Duangjit Taveesri, it is a very fine example of modern work.

An ethnic variety of this is the *pha prae wai*, worn by Phu Tai women from the northeastern provinces of Kalasin, Mukdahan and Ubon Ratchathani. It is also in silk (a speciality of the northeast) with complex supplementary-weft patterns in bright colours, and worn over the breasts as a type of sleeveless camisole. The men's scarf, also visible in the mural here (see also page 136), was normally plainer in design, but some fine decorative designs remain, including the Lanna *sabai* on right, a ceremonial scarf known as a *pha khan kaw si gor* from Nan Province. It is some 60 years old and from the same collection.

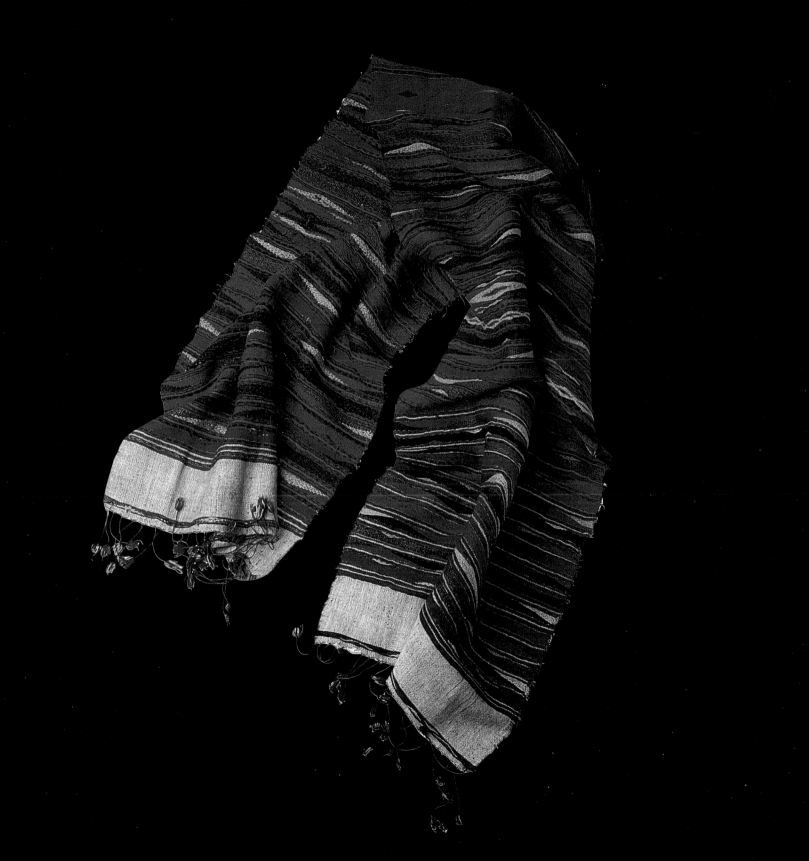

Wicker balls

ตะกร้อ
takraw

From Burma down to Malaysia and up to the Philippines, this ingeniously constructed ball of woven rattan is basic equipment for one of the most popular games in the region—*takraw*. Claimed by all these countries to be their national game (naturally, Thais dispute the others' claims!), it consists in its simplest form of a contest, between two teams, in which the ball is volleyed across a net into the opponents' court without the use of hands or arms. There is no limit to the number of contacts each player can make with the ball: it can be kicked or headed several times to keep it aloft and prepare it for the final delivery.

And what deliveries! Style is important in this game, and spectacular kicks are demanded by audiences that know this game well. The most famous is that in which the player jumps with his back to the net, rotates in the air and kicks the *takraw* over the shoulder opposite from the kicking foot. In international terminology (the game is certainly now played internationally), this is the Roll Spike.

Although the ball is made from locally available materials in a simple and economic design, it contains some surprisingly sophisticated features. What may not be immediately apparent, but was discovered by Professor Buckminster Fuller, is that the *takraw* is in fact a geodesic structure closely related to the domes he made famous.

Throughout rural Thailand, where the game is played everywhere, the *takraw* is still made from woven rattan, though in international sport most players now use woven synthetic (plastic) balls, invented in 1982 by a Thai engineer. The rattan balls range in weight from about 140 g to 200 g (0.3–0.4 lbs); the heavier ones, though they need more kicking force, have more spring and are less affected by wind. Also, the tighter the weave, the more spring, bounce and speed.

The method of construction is ideally suited to the purpose of a light, springy ball: a three-way weave, which is also a common technique in basketry. Triangulated structures like this are extraordinarily efficient, with a very high strength-to-weight ratio, and the foundation is the rigidity of the triangle combined with the compressive strength of a tensile material like rattan.

This is how the *takraw* is related to the geodesic dome, which is a part-sphere made up of a complex network of triangles. According to Buckminster Fuller, this three-way grid distributes stress evenly to all members of the entire structure and hence is extremely strong, enclosing the most volume with the least amount of surface. By following the edges of the triangles, a sphere can be symmetrically divided by a number of great circles, which are the largest circles that can be drawn around a sphere, like lines of longitude around the Earth (hence the term geodesic, from Latin, meaning "earth dividing"). The bands of rattan forming the *takraw* are intersecting great circles.

Thai architect Sumet Jumsai, who analysed this comparison between the *takraw* and architectural structures, noted a more gruesome development during the Ayutthaya period. An over-sized *takraw*, large enough to contain a man, was made and, as punishment, a criminal would be put inside and the *takraw* given to an elephant to kick around. Because of the geometry involved, such a jumbo *takraw* would have needed a higher frequency of latticing, more inter-triangulated surfaces, and so a closer approximation to a true sphere.

Selected Bibliography

Bhilasri, Professor S., *Thai Lacquer.* Bangkok:
Fine Arts Department, 1989.

Bhilasri, Professor S., *Thai Buddhist Art (Architecture).*
Bangkok: Fine Arts Department, 1963.

Brown, R., *The Ceramics of South-East Asia.*
Oxford in Asia, 1988.

Brownrigg, H., *Betel Cutters.* Stuttgart: Editions Hansjörg
Mayer, 1991.

Charernsupkul, A., *The Elements of Thai Architecture.*
Bangkok: Satri Sarn, 1978.

Clewley, J., "The Many Sounds of Siam", in *World Music.*
London: Rough Guides, 1994.

Conway, S., *Thai Textiles.* Bangkok: Asia Books, 1992.

Dumarçay, J., *The House in South-East Asia.* Singapore:
Oxford University Press, 1987.

Faculty of Painting and Sculpture (ed.), *The Folk Art of
Uthong, Sukhothai, Bangkok.* Bangkok: Silpakorn
University, 1996.

Farrelly, D., *The Book of Bamboo.* London: Thames &
Hudson, 1996.

Fraser-Lu, S., *Silverware of South-East Asia.* Singapore:
Oxford University Press, 1989.

Frédéric, L., *Buddhism.* Paris: Flammarion, 1995.

Gosling, B., *Sukhothai: Its History, Culture and Art.*
Singapore: Oxford University Press, 1991.

Graham, M. and Winkler, M., *Thai Coins.* Bangkok:
Finance One Ltd.,1992

Hallet, H., *A Thousand Miles on an Elephant in the Shan
States.* Bangkok: White Lotus, 1988.

Jumsai, S., *Naga: Cultural Origins in Siam and the West
Pacific.* Singapore: Oxford University Press, 1988.

Kangkananda, M., *Folk Crafts in Thailand.* Bangkok:
Silpakorn University, 1981.

Krug, S. and Duboff, S., *The Kamthieng House.* Bangkok:
Siam Society, 1982.

La Loubère, Simon de, *A New Historical Relation of the
Kingdom of Siam.* Originally published in London, 1693.

Lair, R., *Gone Astray: The Care and Management of the
Asian Elephant in Domesticity.* Rome: FAO, 1997.

Leesuwan, V., *Thai Culture and Heritage.* Bangkok:
The Office of the National Culture Commission, Ministry
of Education,1981.

Leesuwan, V., *Thai Folk Craft.* Bangkok: The Office of the
National Culture Commission, Ministry of Education,1981.

Leesuwan, V., *Thai Traditional Crafts.* Bangkok:
The Office of the National Culture Commission, Ministry
of Education, 1981.

Moore, E., Stott, P., Suryavudh, S. and Freeman, M., *Ancient
Capitals of Thailand.* Bangkok: River Books, 1996.

National Identity Board (ed.), *Thai Life: Thai Folk Art and
Crafts.* Bangkok: The Prime Minister's Office, 1998.

National Museum Division (ed.), *Thai Minor Arts.* Bangkok:
Fine Arts Department, 1993.

Panjabhan, N., *Silverware in Thailand.* Bangkok: Rerngrom
Publishing, 1991.

Panjabhan, N., Wichienkeeo, A. and Na Nakhon Phanom, S.,
The Charm of Lanna Wood Carving and *The Art of Thai
Wood Carving.* Bangkok: Rerngrom Publishing, 1994.

Pattaratorn, C., *Votive Tablets in Thailand.* Kuala Lumpur:
Oxford University Press, 1997.

Phothisuntr, W., *The Art of Mother of Pearl Inlay.*
Bangkok, 1981.

Prangwatthanakun, S. and Naenna, P., *Chiangmai's Textile
Heritage.*

Shan, J. C., *Northern Thai Ceramics.* Oxford, 1981.

Suksri, N. and Freeman, M., *The Grand Palace.* Bangkok:
River Books, 1998.

Trakullertsathien, C., *The Lost Art of Norah Performance.*
Bangkok: Bangkok Post, Outlook, 2000.

Van Beek, S. and Tettoni, L., *The Arts of Thailand.*
Hong Kong: Periplus, 1999.

Wickremesinghe, K. D. P., *The Biography of the Buddha.*
Colombo, 1972.

Wyatt, D. K., *Thailand: A Short History.* New Haven:
Yale University Press, 1984.

Yopho, D., *Thai Musical Instruments.* Bangkok:
Department of Fine Arts, 1957.

Sources

The author and photographer would like to thank the
following for their assistance:

M.R. Narisa Chakrabongse
Anongnart Ulapathorn
Mimi Lipton
William Booth
Neyla Freeman

Lanna
3 Denbigh Road
London W11 2SJ
tel: +44 20 7229 6765
fax: +44 20 7792 0027

Piece of Art
River City
Room 451, 4th Floor
23 Trok Rongnamkaeng Road
Smapantawong
Bangkok 10100
tel: +66 2 237 0077
fax: +66 2 237 0078 ext. 451

Rama Antiques
1238/1–2 corner Soi 36
New Road
Bangkok 10500
tel: +66 2 235 7991
fax: +66 2 236 8104
e-mail: ramaart@thaimail.com

Jim Thompson Thai Silk Company
9 Surawong Road
Bangkok 10500
tel: +66 2 632 8100
fax: +66 2 236 6777
email: office@jimthompson.com

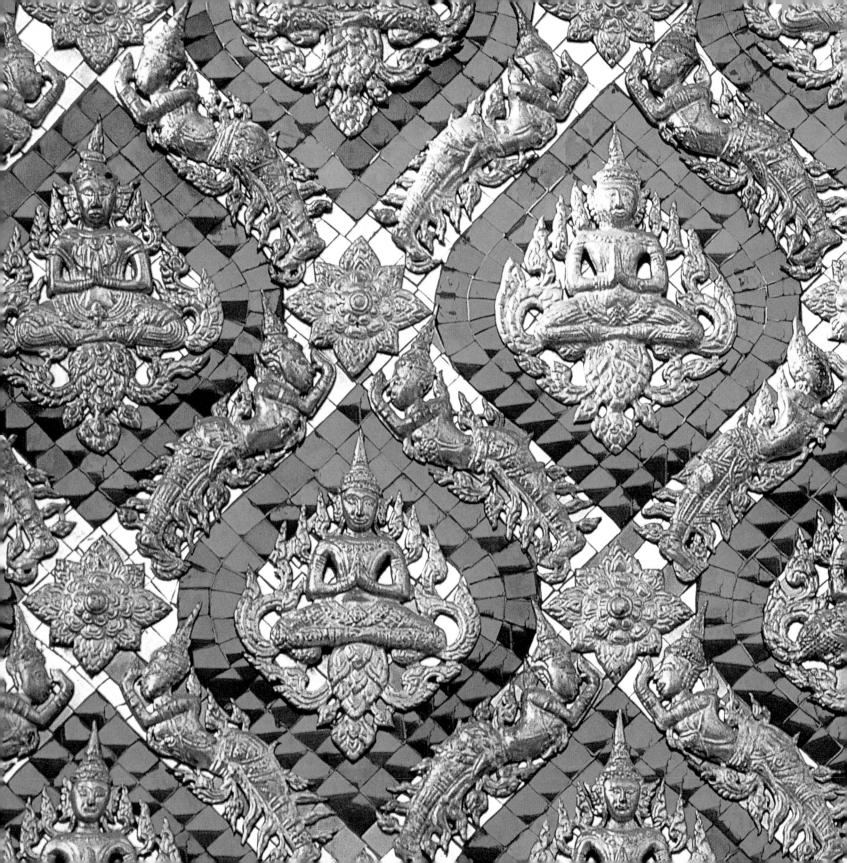